I Wish I Could Fly

I Wish I Could Fly

By Judy Gordon Morrow

Broadman & Holman Publishers
Nashville, Tennessee

Printed in the United States of America

0-8054-1662-5

Published by Broadman & Holman Publishers, Nashville, Tennessee
Editorial Team: Vicki Crumpton, Janis Whipple, Kim Overcash
Page Design: Paul T. Gant Art & Design
Typesetting: PerfecType, Nashville, Tennessee

Dewey Decimal Classification: 081
Subject Heading: CHILDREN—QUOTATIONS / WISHES
Library of Congress Card Catalog Number: 98-37762

Library of Congress Cataloging-in-Publication Data

Morrow, Judy Gordon
I wish I could fly : when kids make a wish / [compiled and edited by] Judy Gordon Morrow.
p. cm.
ISBN 0-8054-1662-5 (pbk.)
1. Children—Quotations. 2. Wishes. I. Title.
PN6328.C5M671999
081'.083—dc21

98-37762
CIP

1 2 3 4 5 03 02 01 00 99

Dedication

For my E-mail writers' group, "One Heart," with love and appreciation. I wish everyone could know love and encouragement like yours.

Acknowledgments

Thank you to the following teachers and parents who helped gather the children's responses:

Virginia Ball
Pat Boyer
Ruth Carnell
Yvonne Casalnuovo
Jason Clark
Becky Cobb
Pat Crosby
Madeline D'Andrea
Bob Dickinson
Darla Draper
Brenda Farley
Nancy Gordon
Tricia Goyer
Michele Graham
Andrea Grinnell
Sue Gutierrez
Susan Hagwood
Julie Hochrein
Joy Jackson
Susan Jackson

Cathy Jones
Jan Kern
Pauline Kimmel
Holly La Chappel
Kathy Manus
Cindy Martinusen
Janet Holm McHenry
Annette McTighe
Shelly Morrow
Vicki Murray
Christine Peters
Loretta Ramirez
Michael Rodriguez
JoAnne Rotta
Susan Salucci
Betsy Schaffer
Ellen Schwartz
Diane Seibel
Don Shaw
Nancy Sipe
Adrienne Stenson
Pamela Townsend
Joan Turner
Susanne Vaughn
Mary Vossler
Donna Weber
Jeanne Williams

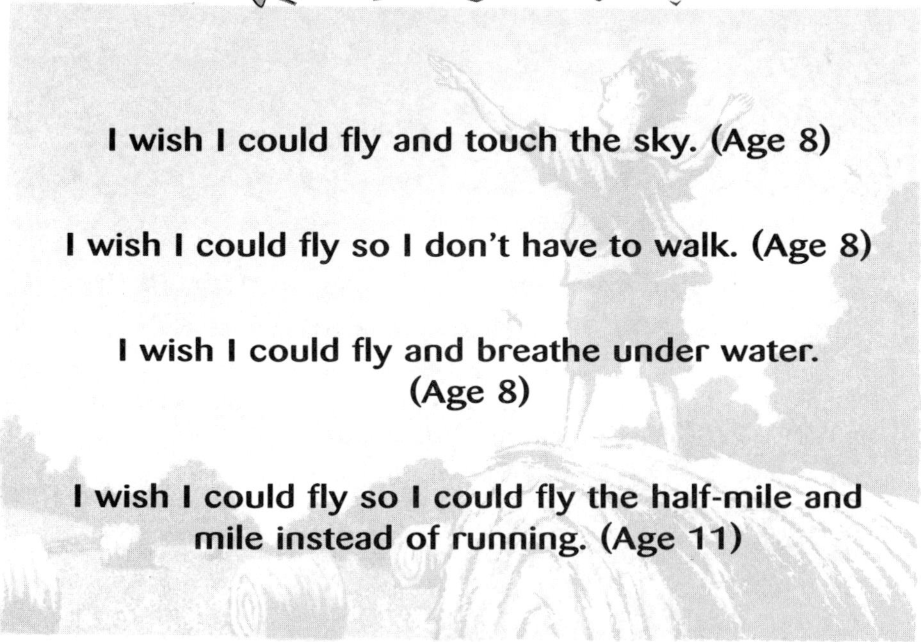

I wish I could fly and touch the sky. (Age 8)

I wish I could fly so I don't have to walk. (Age 8)

I wish I could fly and breathe under water. (Age 8)

I wish I could fly so I could fly the half-mile and mile instead of running. (Age 11)

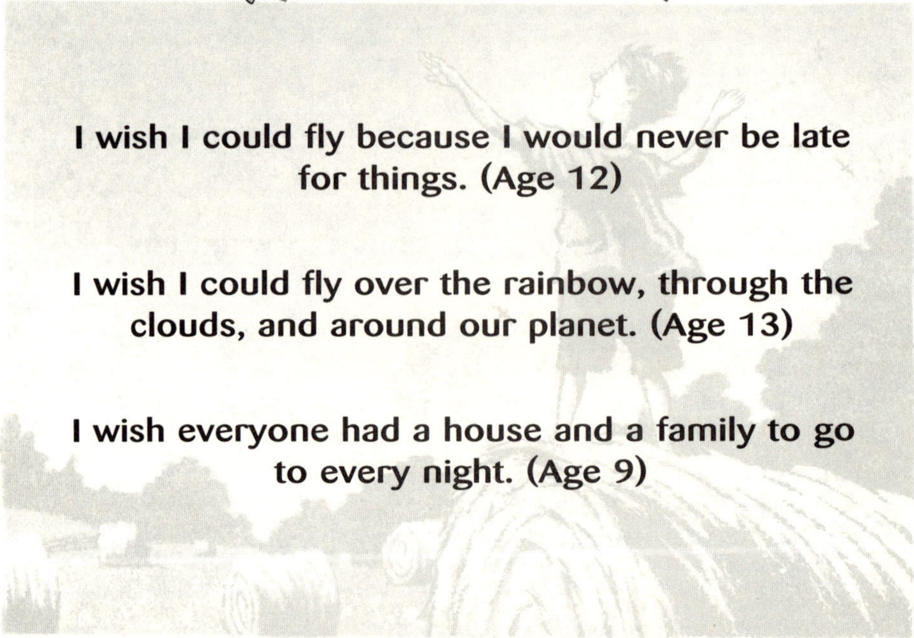

I wish I could fly because I would never be late for things. (Age 12)

I wish I could fly over the rainbow, through the clouds, and around our planet. (Age 13)

I wish everyone had a house and a family to go to every night. (Age 9)

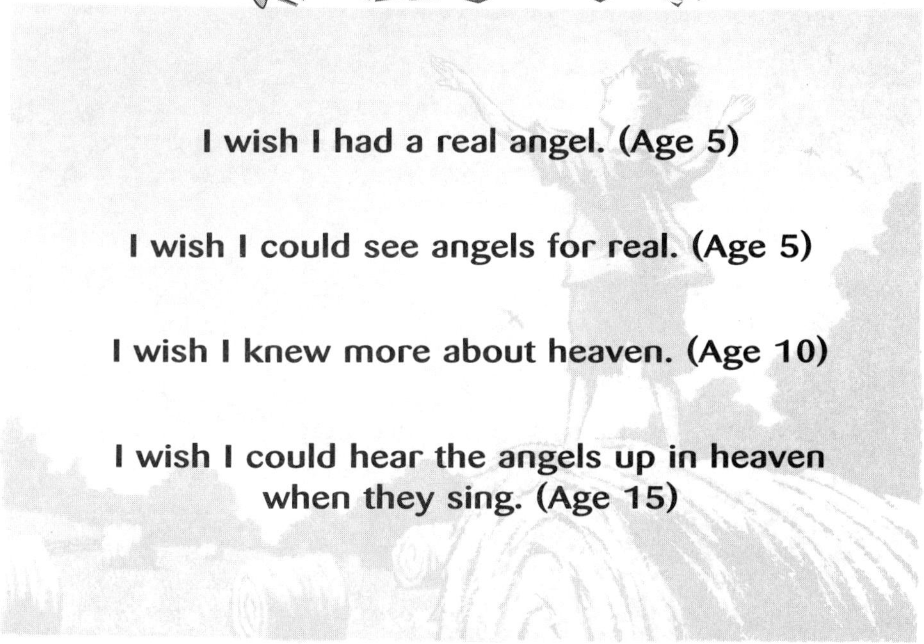

I wish I had a real angel. (Age 5)

I wish I could see angels for real. (Age 5)

I wish I knew more about heaven. (Age 10)

I wish I could hear the angels up in heaven when they sing. (Age 15)

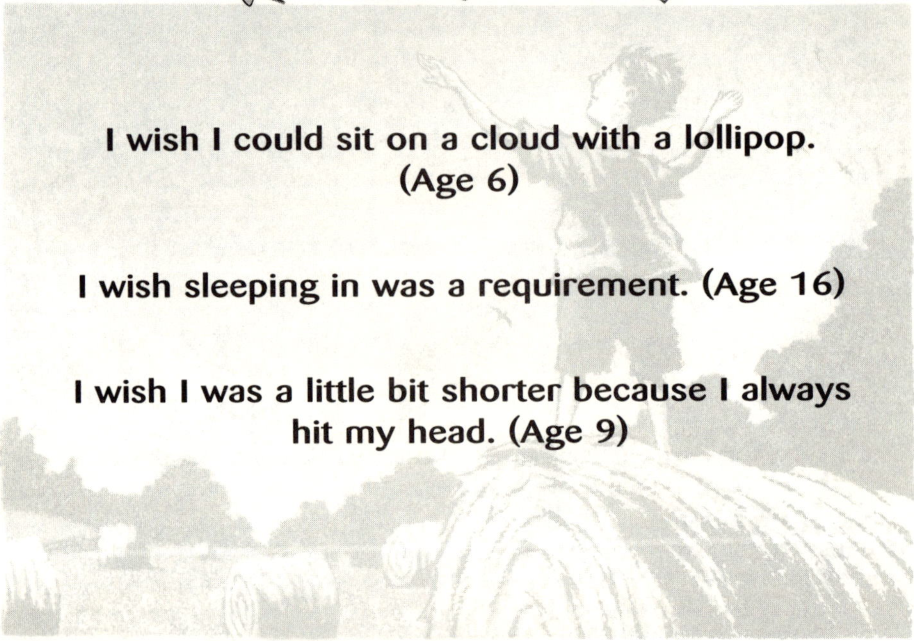

I wish I could sit on a cloud with a lollipop.
(Age 6)

I wish sleeping in was a requirement. (Age 16)

I wish I was a little bit shorter because I always hit my head. (Age 9)

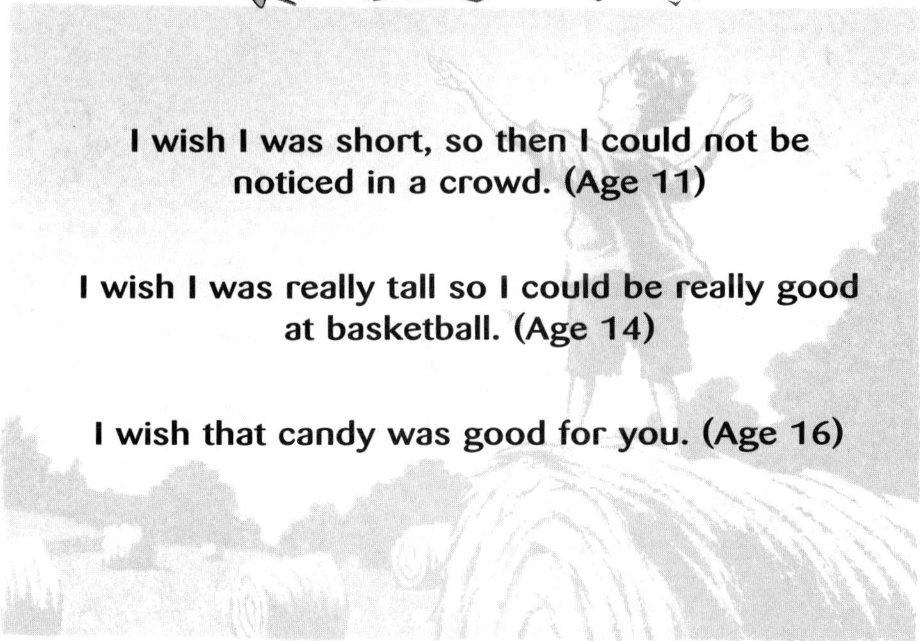

I wish I was short, so then I could not be noticed in a crowd. (Age 11)

I wish I was really tall so I could be really good at basketball. (Age 14)

I wish that candy was good for you. (Age 16)

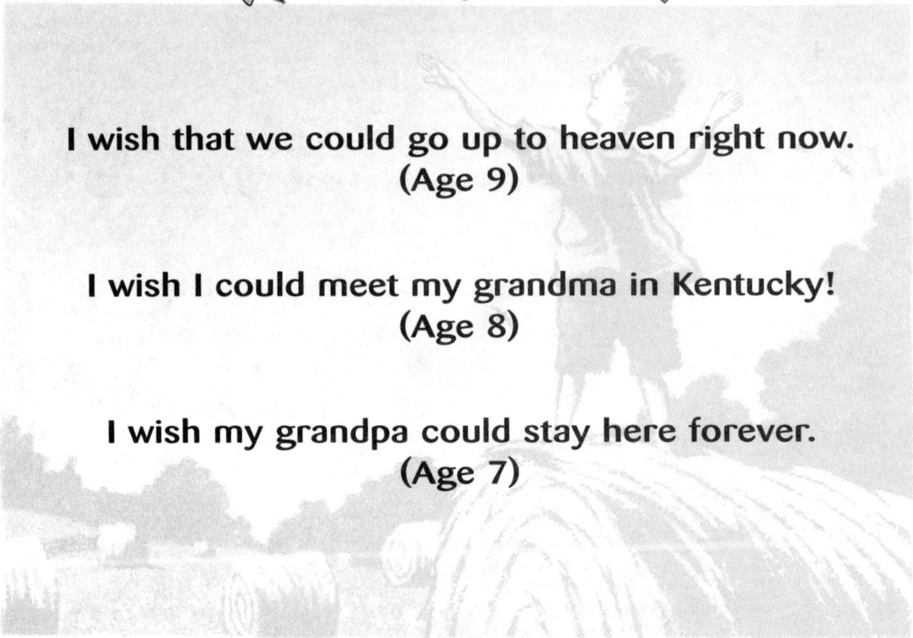

I wish that we could go up to heaven right now.
(Age 9)

I wish I could meet my grandma in Kentucky!
(Age 8)

I wish my grandpa could stay here forever.
(Age 7)

I wish everyone will someday walk hand in hand like in Martin Luther King Jr.'s dream. (Age 8)

I wish that all black and white people would play together and be friends. (Age 5)

I wish nobody would have to go through cancer. (Age 14)

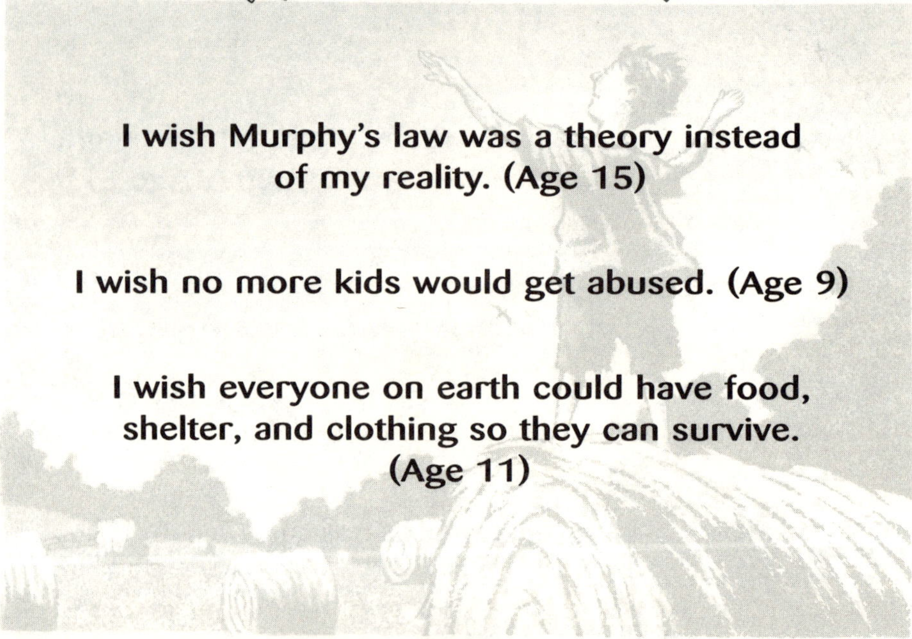

I wish Murphy's law was a theory instead of my reality. (Age 15)

I wish no more kids would get abused. (Age 9)

I wish everyone on earth could have food, shelter, and clothing so they can survive. (Age 11)

I wish the world was made out of chocolate. (Age 10)

I wish for the world to be pizza. (Age 7)

I wish that the world would be perfect just like God. (Age 9)

I wish that life was as easy as pie. (Age 17)

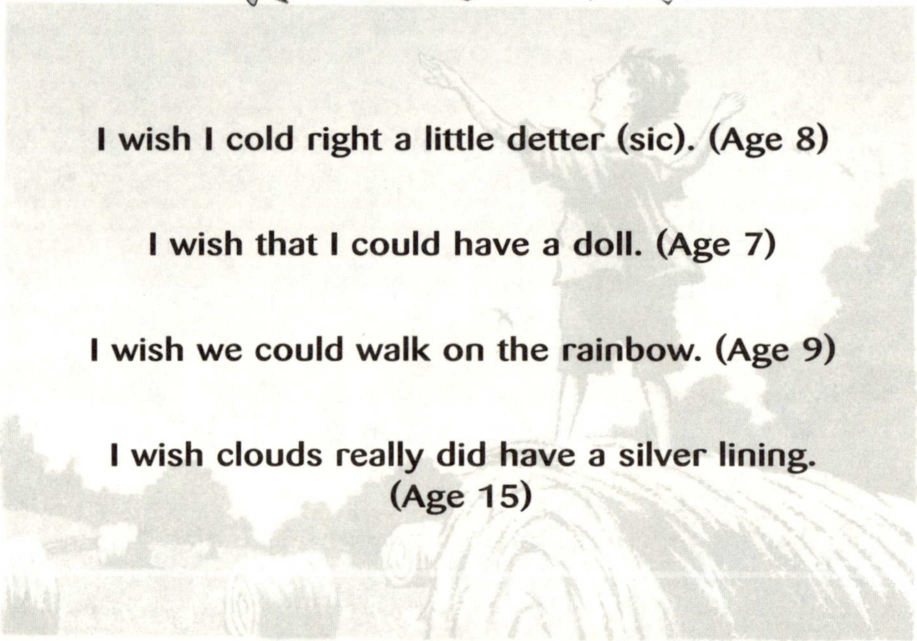

I wish I cold right a little detter (sic). (Age 8)

I wish that I could have a doll. (Age 7)

I wish we could walk on the rainbow. (Age 9)

I wish clouds really did have a silver lining.
(Age 15)

I wish I could go around the world in a hot air balloon. (Age 10)

I wish I could sail on the creek and all the way to the ocean, fishing all the way. (Age 7)

I wish I knew what to wish for. (Age 16)

I wish I had more books. (Age 9)

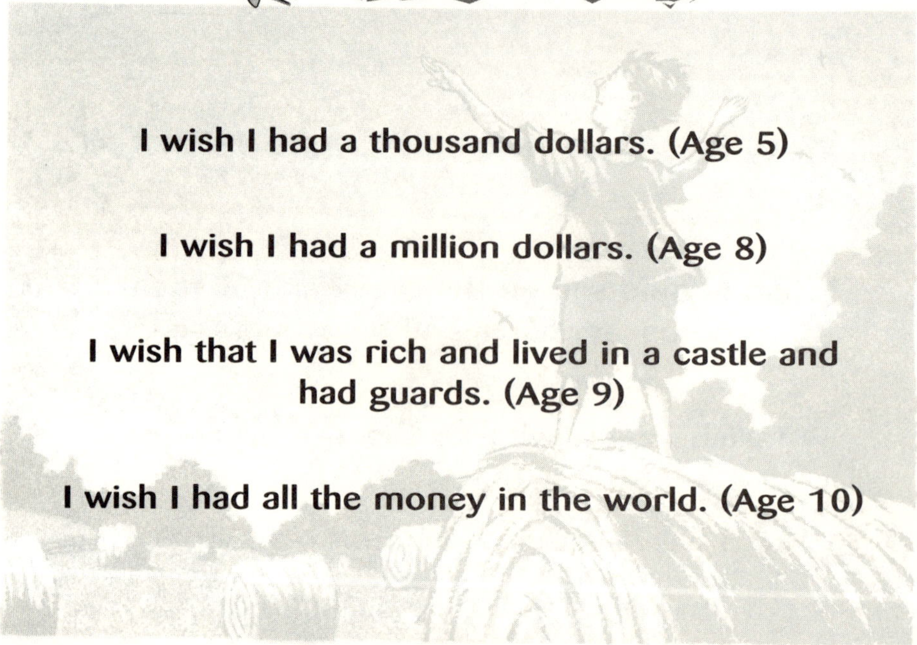

I wish I had a thousand dollars. (Age 5)

I wish I had a million dollars. (Age 8)

I wish that I was rich and lived in a castle and had guards. (Age 9)

I wish I had all the money in the world. (Age 10)

I wish money grew on trees. (Age 11)

I wish that I had five billion dollars, so I could pay off my parents' bills and buy Dad a Camaro. Also, so I could go to college. (Age 12)

I wish that money did not exist. (Age 18)

I wish that everyone could stop thinking about themselves and money. (Age 11)

I wish everybody would realize that life and health are a lot more important than money and looks. (Age 11)

I wish that everyone had a lot of toys. (Age 5)

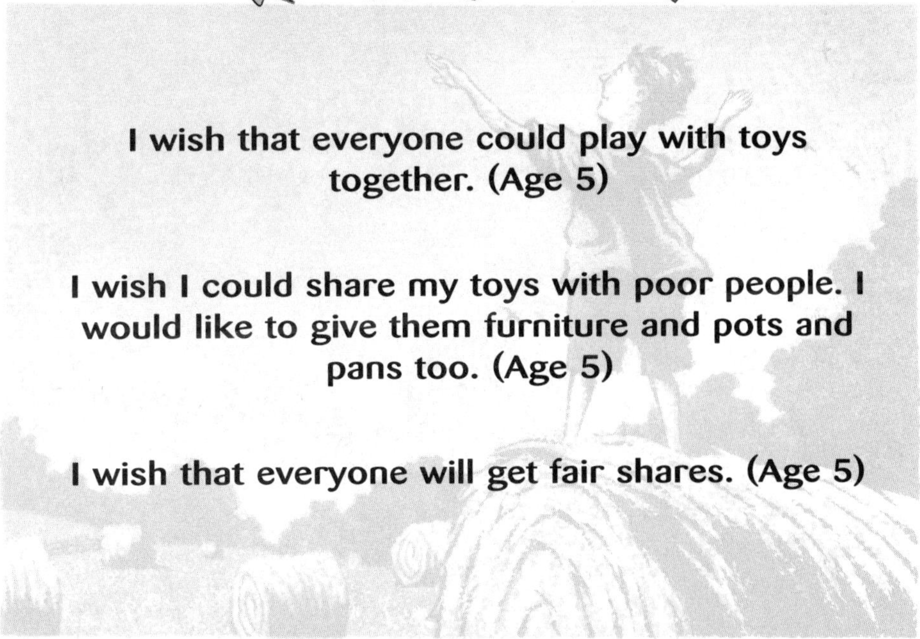

I wish that everyone could play with toys together. (Age 5)

I wish I could share my toys with poor people. I would like to give them furniture and pots and pans too. (Age 5)

I wish that everyone will get fair shares. (Age 5)

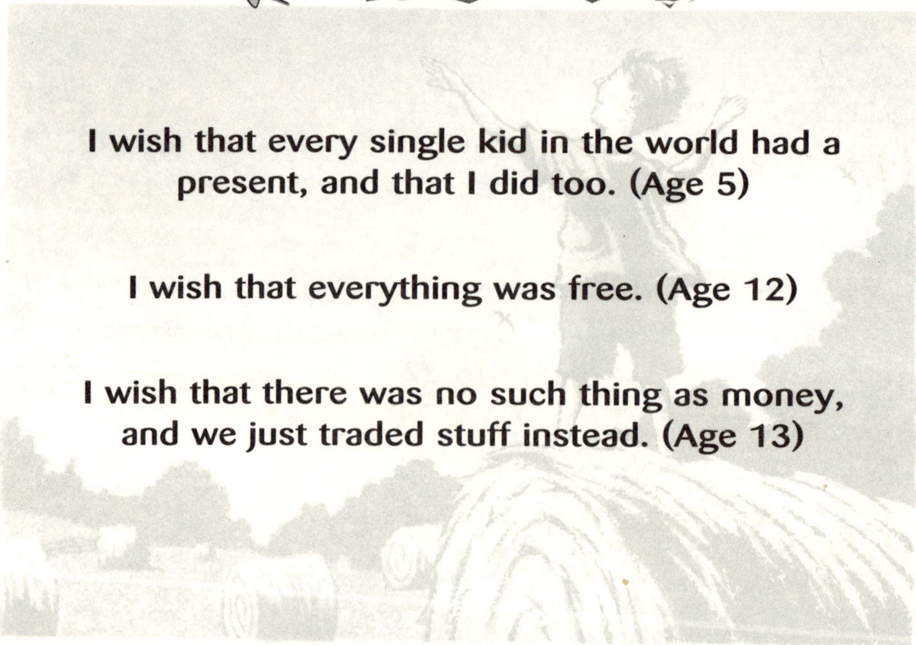

I wish that every single kid in the world had a present, and that I did too. (Age 5)

I wish that everything was free. (Age 12)

I wish that there was no such thing as money, and we just traded stuff instead. (Age 13)

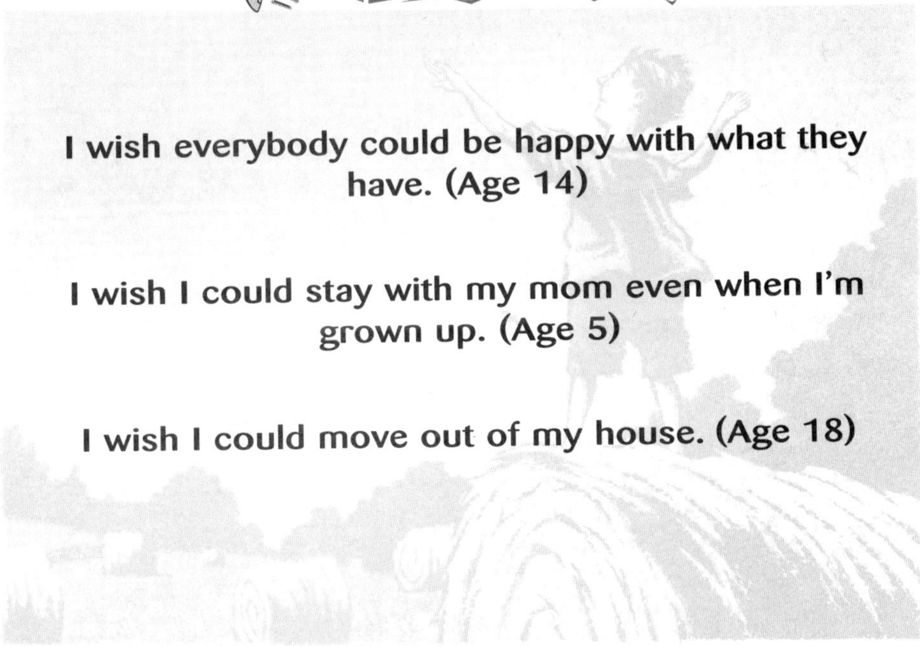

I wish everybody could be happy with what they have. (Age 14)

I wish I could stay with my mom even when I'm grown up. (Age 5)

I wish I could move out of my house. (Age 18)

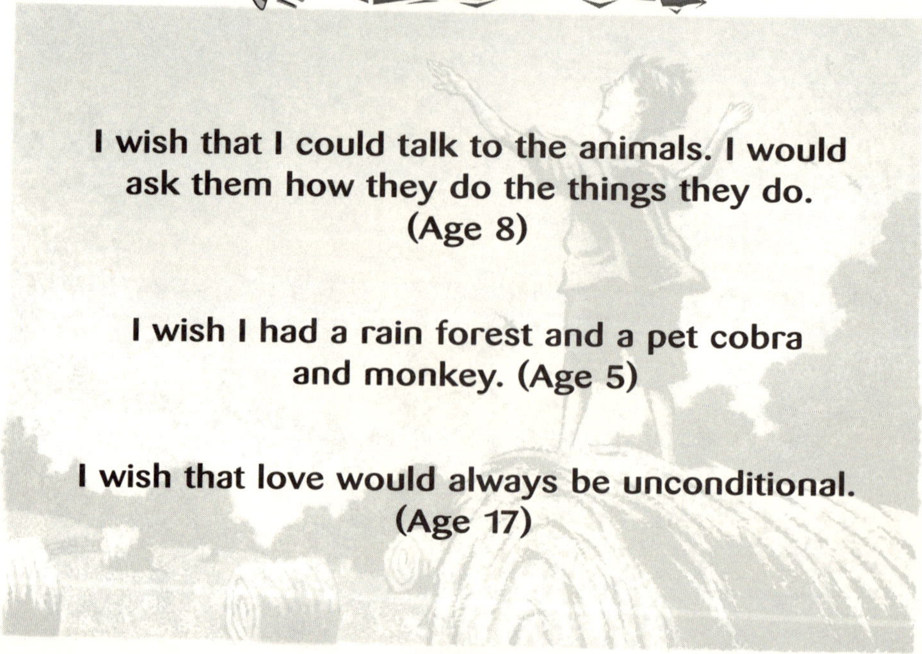

I wish that I could talk to the animals. I would ask them how they do the things they do. (Age 8)

I wish I had a rain forest and a pet cobra and monkey. (Age 5)

I wish that love would always be unconditional. (Age 17)

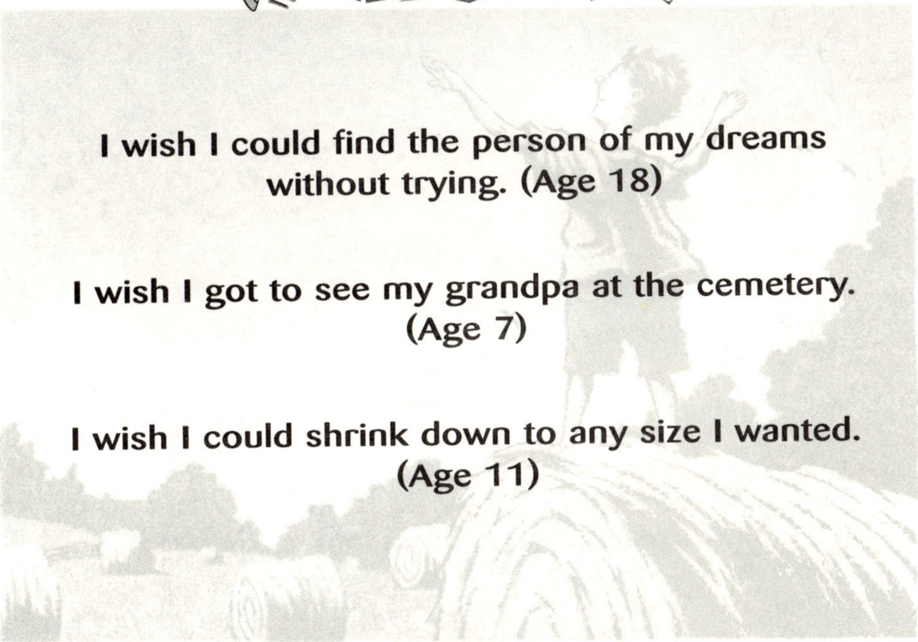

I wish I could find the person of my dreams without trying. (Age 18)

I wish I got to see my grandpa at the cemetery. (Age 7)

I wish I could shrink down to any size I wanted. (Age 11)

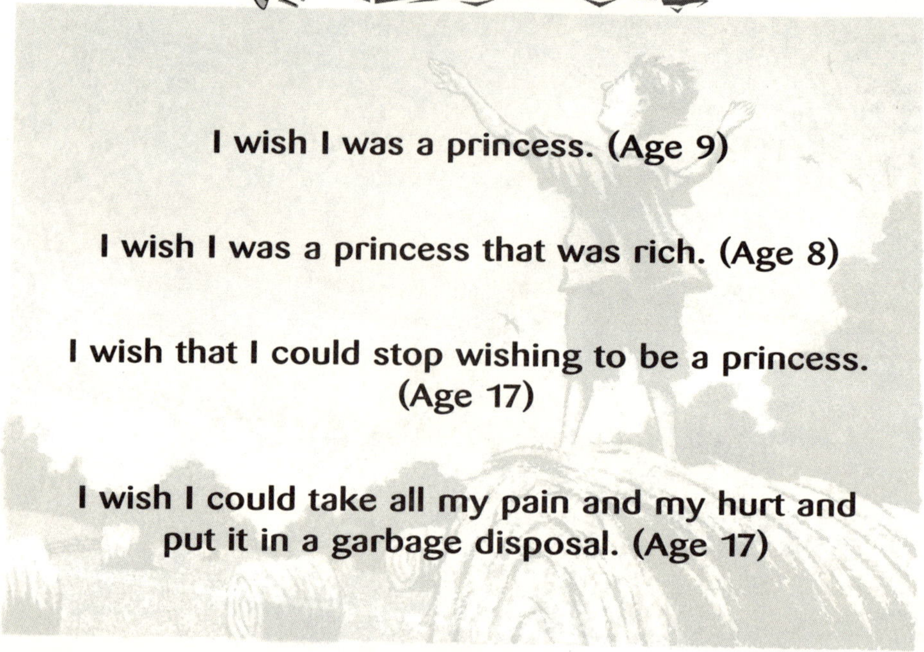

I wish I was a princess. (Age 9)

I wish I was a princess that was rich. (Age 8)

I wish that I could stop wishing to be a princess. (Age 17)

I wish I could take all my pain and my hurt and put it in a garbage disposal. (Age 17)

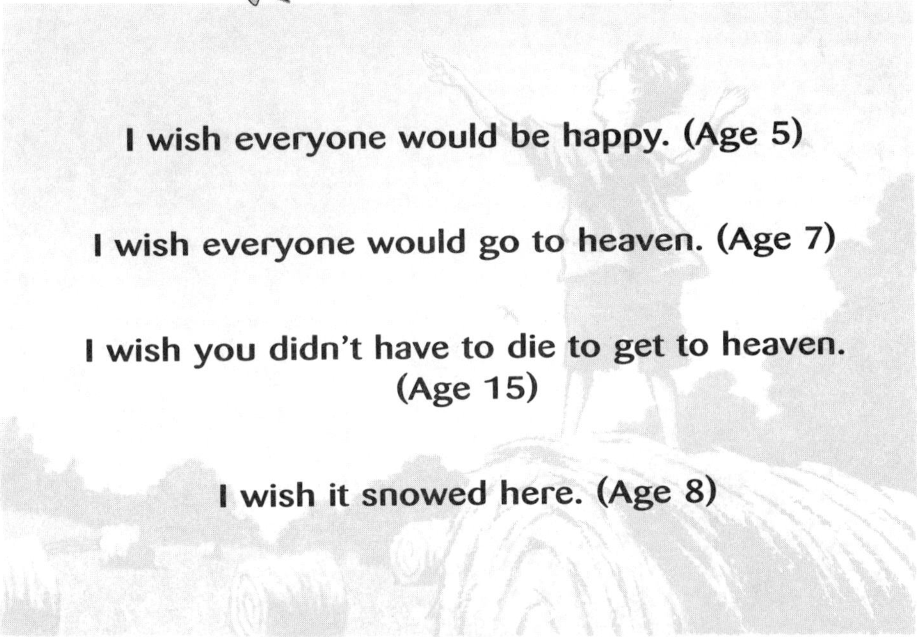

I wish everyone would be happy. (Age 5)

I wish everyone would go to heaven. (Age 7)

I wish you didn't have to die to get to heaven. (Age 15)

I wish it snowed here. (Age 8)

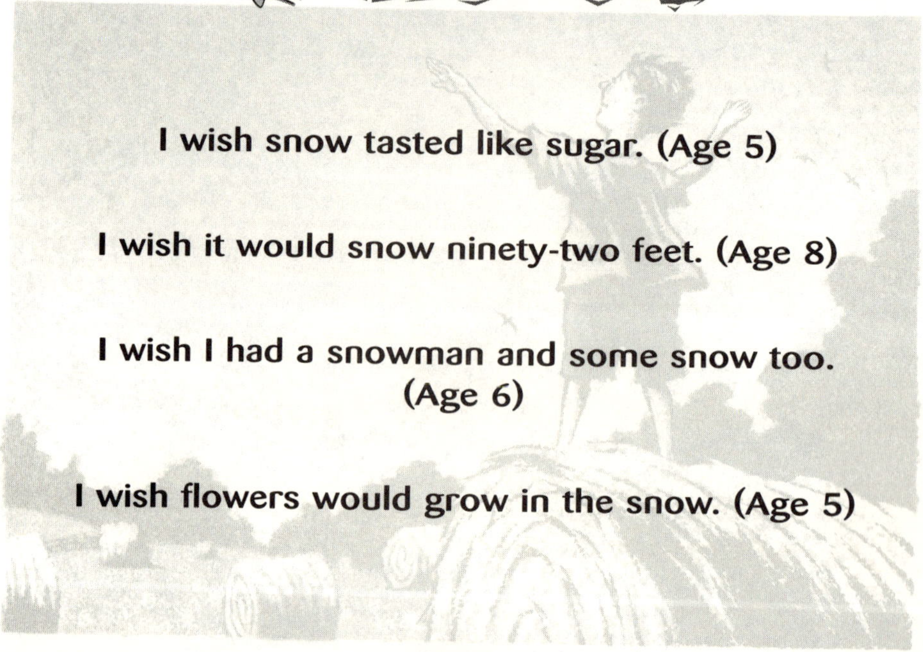

I wish snow tasted like sugar. (Age 5)

I wish it would snow ninety-two feet. (Age 8)

I wish I had a snowman and some snow too. (Age 6)

I wish flowers would grow in the snow. (Age 5)

I wish the sky could be blue when it snows because it would be so pretty. (Age 15)

I wish every day was a snow day. (Age 16)

I wish my teacher could come snowboarding with me. (Age 8)

I wish to marry my teacher. (Age 5)

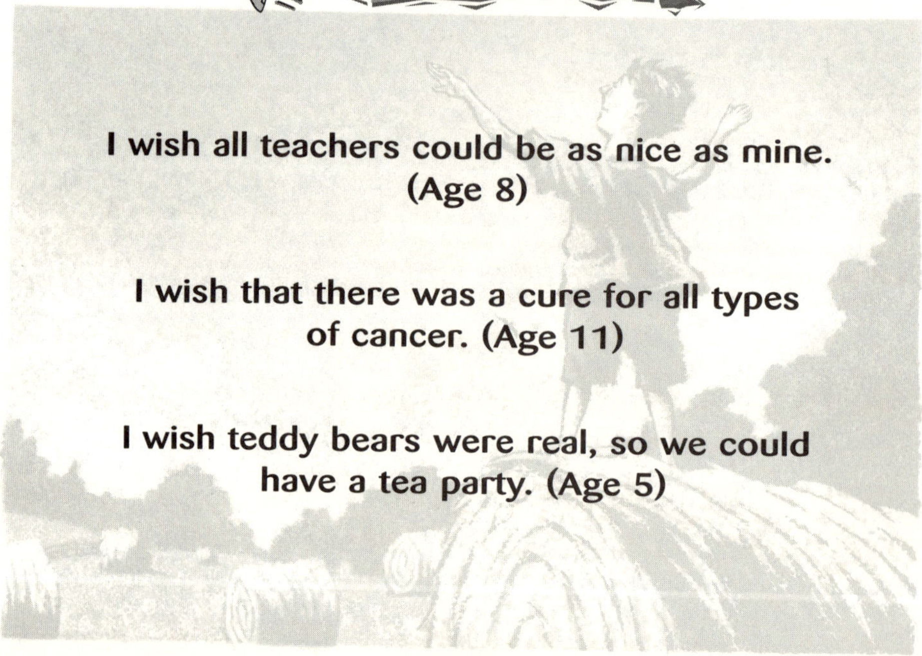

I wish all teachers could be as nice as mine. (Age 8)

I wish that there was a cure for all types of cancer. (Age 11)

I wish teddy bears were real, so we could have a tea party. (Age 5)

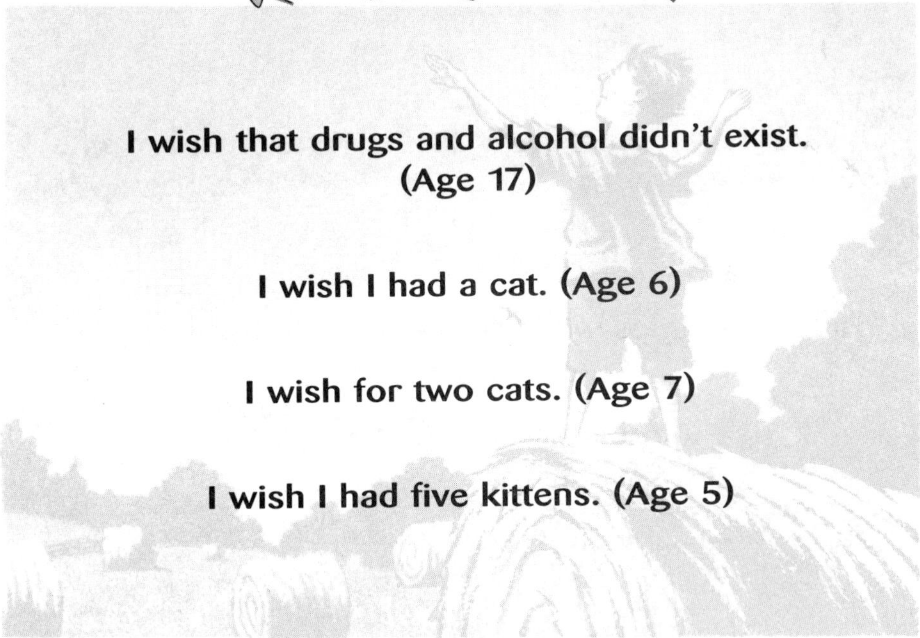

I wish that drugs and alcohol didn't exist. (Age 17)

I wish I had a cat. (Age 6)

I wish for two cats. (Age 7)

I wish I had five kittens. (Age 5)

I wish I had a kitty so I do not have to share the cat. I want my cat to be a girl so it has puppies. (Age 7)

I wish doggies weren't mean to kitties. (Age 5)

I wish that pets would never die. (Age 16)

I wish that my best friend and me could grow up together and live in the same house. (Age 11)

I wish that I could swim like a mermaid. (Age 17)

I wish I was a mermaid to see what's under the sea. (Age 6)

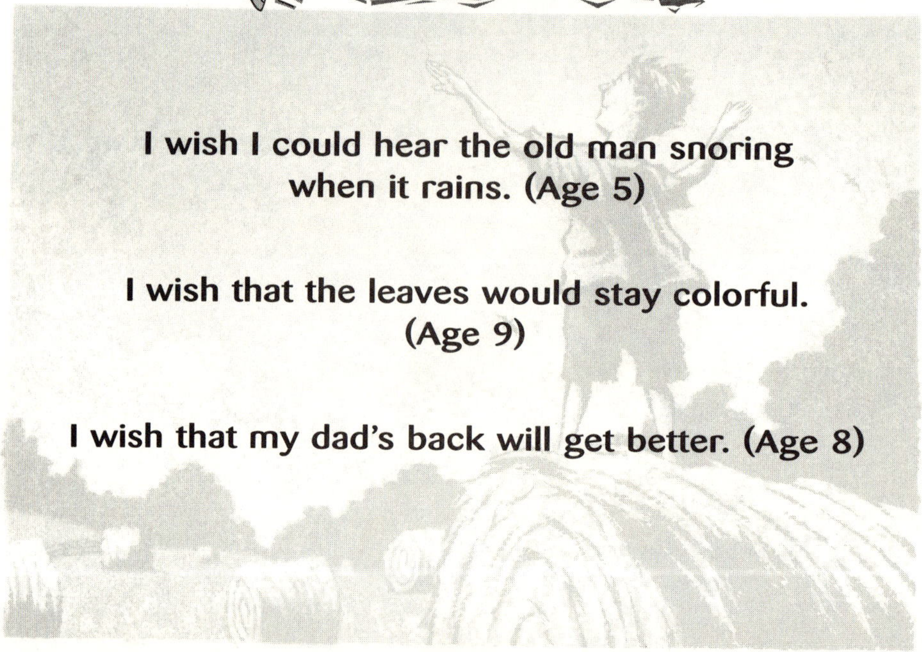

I wish I could hear the old man snoring when it rains. (Age 5)

I wish that the leaves would stay colorful. (Age 9)

I wish that my dad's back will get better. (Age 8)

I wish I had all the answers to life's little problems. (Age 15)

I wish Hawaii was a deserted island. (Age 16)

I wish I wouldn't burp when I drink soda. (Age 5)

I wish my swing set is built. (Age 7)

I wish I could stop doodling. (Age 17)

I wish that the world never comes to an end. (Age 11)

I wish some teachers wouldn't be stereotypical and pick favorite students. (Age 16)

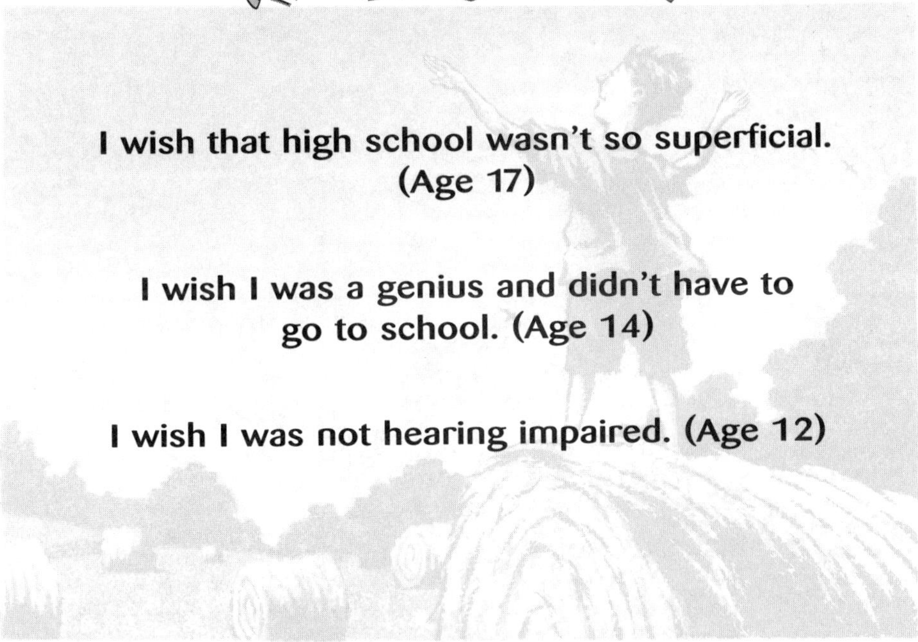

I wish that high school wasn't so superficial. (Age 17)

I wish I was a genius and didn't have to go to school. (Age 14)

I wish I was not hearing impaired. (Age 12)

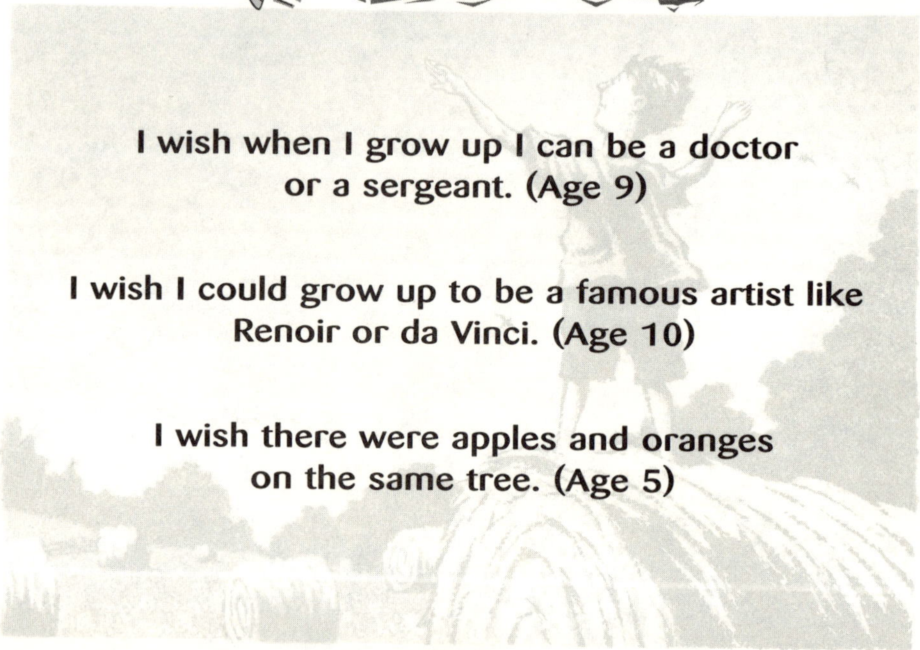

I wish when I grow up I can be a doctor or a sergeant. (Age 9)

I wish I could grow up to be a famous artist like Renoir or da Vinci. (Age 10)

I wish there were apples and oranges on the same tree. (Age 5)

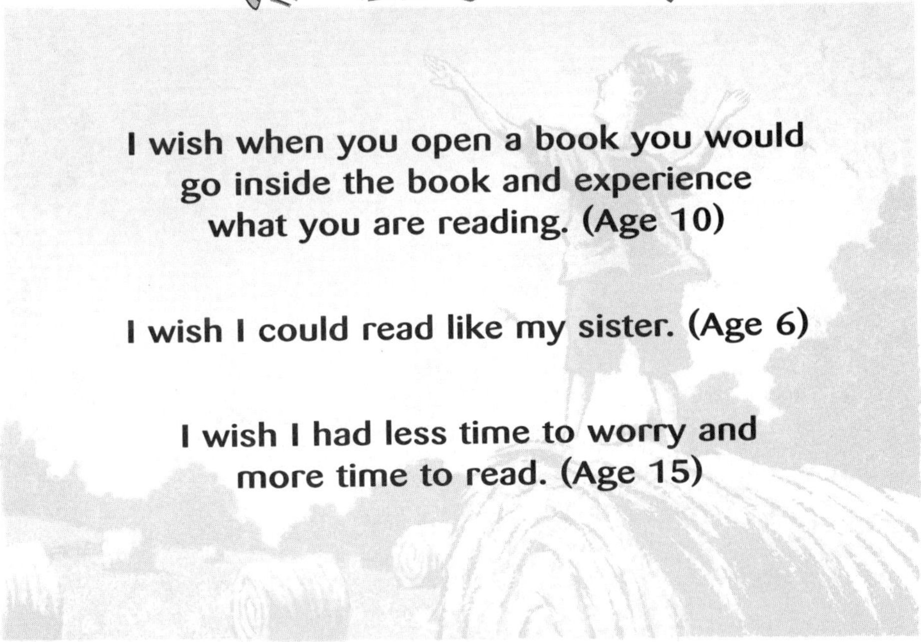

I wish when you open a book you would go inside the book and experience what you are reading. (Age 10)

I wish I could read like my sister. (Age 6)

I wish I had less time to worry and more time to read. (Age 15)

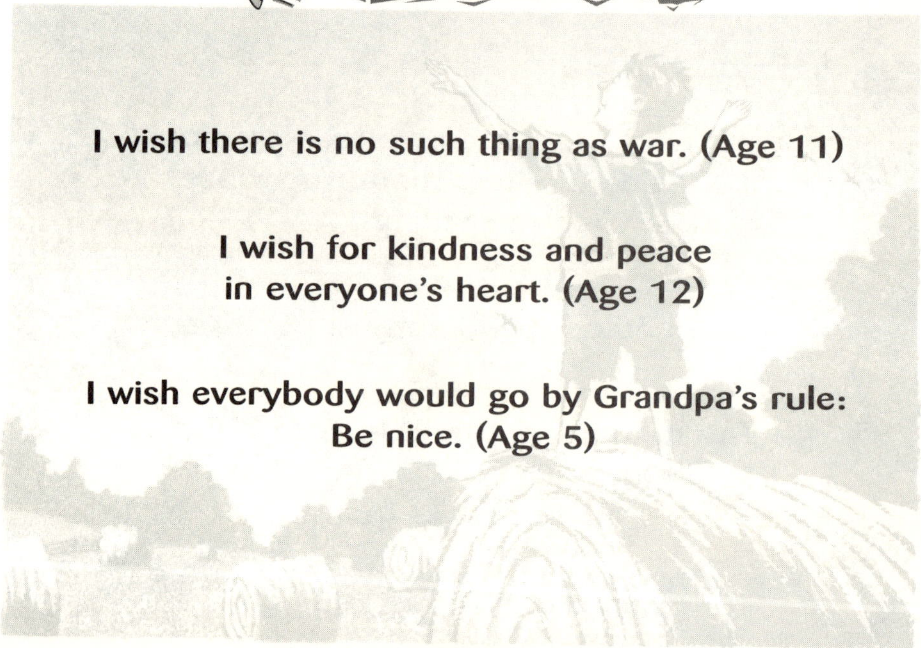

I wish there is no such thing as war. (Age 11)

I wish for kindness and peace
in everyone's heart. (Age 12)

I wish everybody would go by Grandpa's rule:
Be nice. (Age 5)

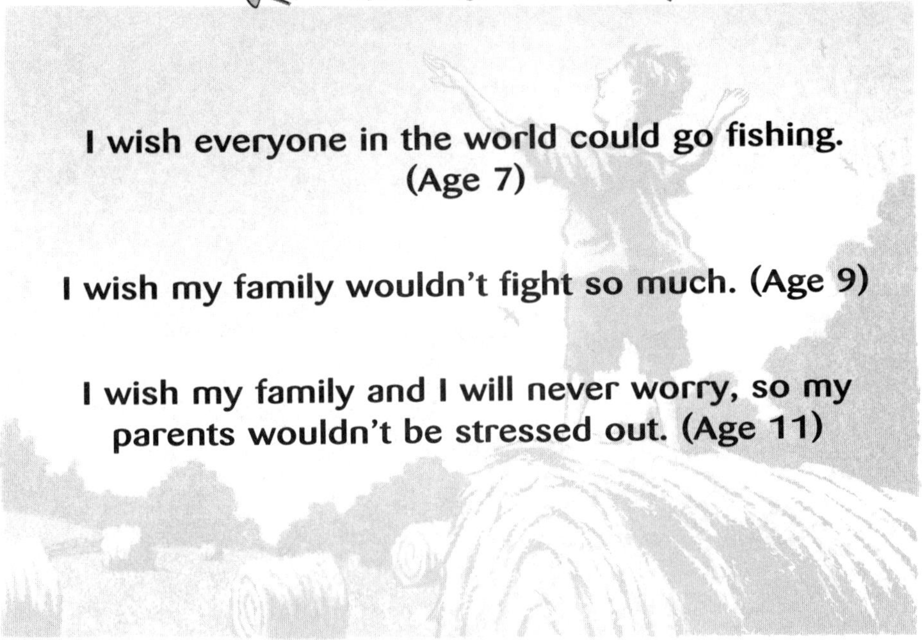

I wish everyone in the world could go fishing.
(Age 7)

I wish my family wouldn't fight so much. (Age 9)

I wish my family and I will never worry, so my parents wouldn't be stressed out. (Age 11)

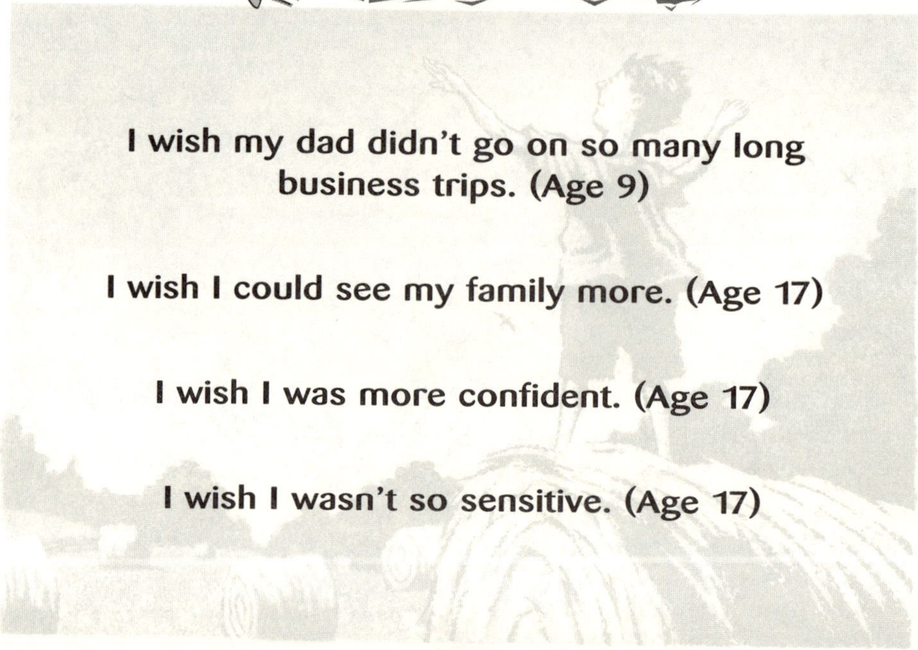

I wish my dad didn't go on so many long business trips. (Age 9)

I wish I could see my family more. (Age 17)

I wish I was more confident. (Age 17)

I wish I wasn't so sensitive. (Age 17)

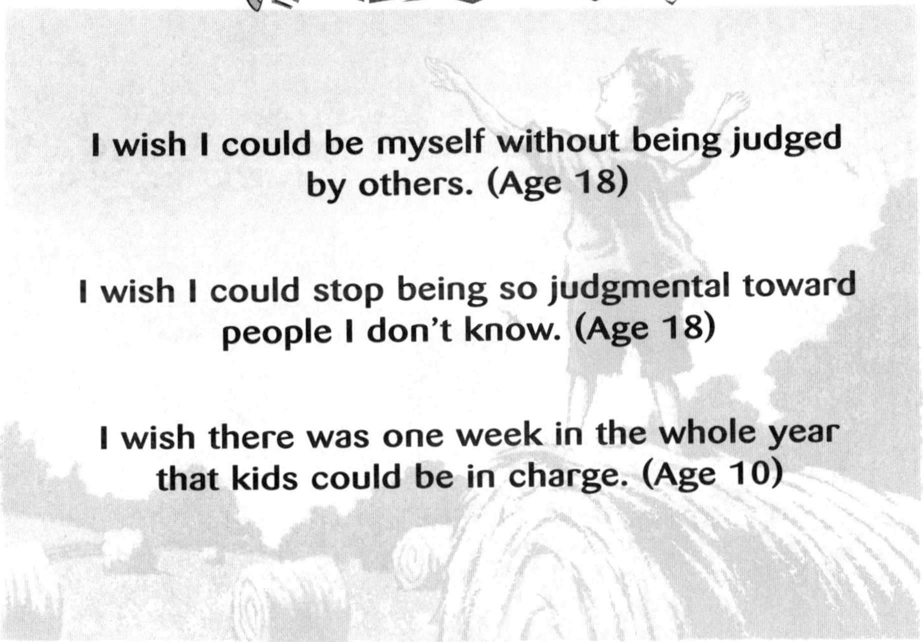

I wish I could be myself without being judged by others. (Age 18)

I wish I could stop being so judgmental toward people I don't know. (Age 18)

I wish there was one week in the whole year that kids could be in charge. (Age 10)

I wish for no wars, no complaining, no fighting—just friendliness between all living things, including animals. (Age 12)

I wish my mom could find her puzzle piece. (Age 5)

I wish the local appliance store's commercials would go off the air. (Age 15)

I wish I could be like my teacher. (Age 8)

I wish I could be a teacher. (Age 8)

I wish I could improve myself enough so that I could improve the world. (Age 14)

I wish that I could hold my breath under water for a long, long time. (Age 9)

I wish that I could swallow knowledge like water.
(Age 17)

I wish I had all the knowledge in the world.
(Age 8)

I wish I had enough money to buy gifts for every teacher in the school. (Age 19)

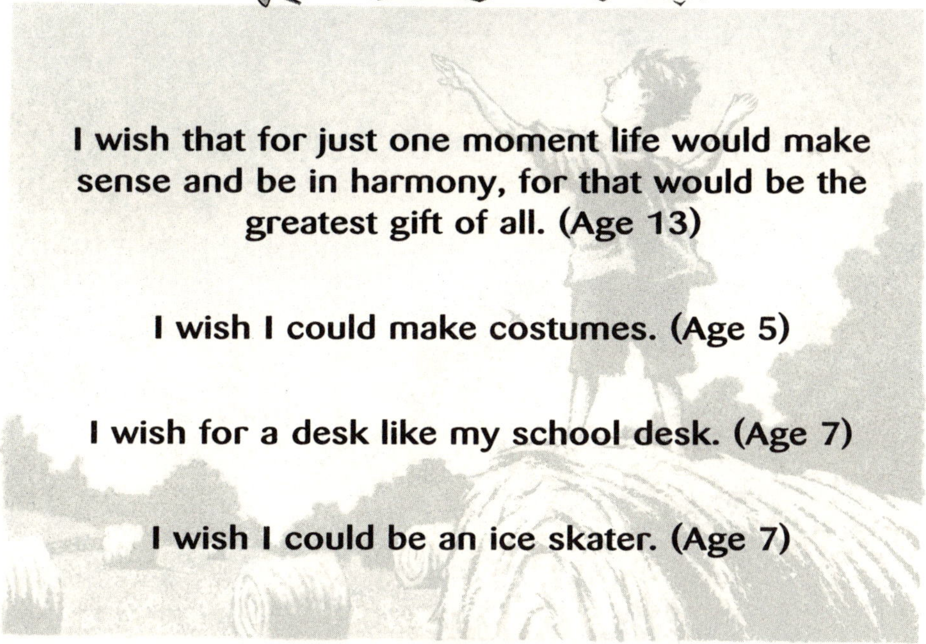

I wish that for just one moment life would make sense and be in harmony, for that would be the greatest gift of all. (Age 13)

I wish I could make costumes. (Age 5)

I wish for a desk like my school desk. (Age 7)

I wish I could be an ice skater. (Age 7)

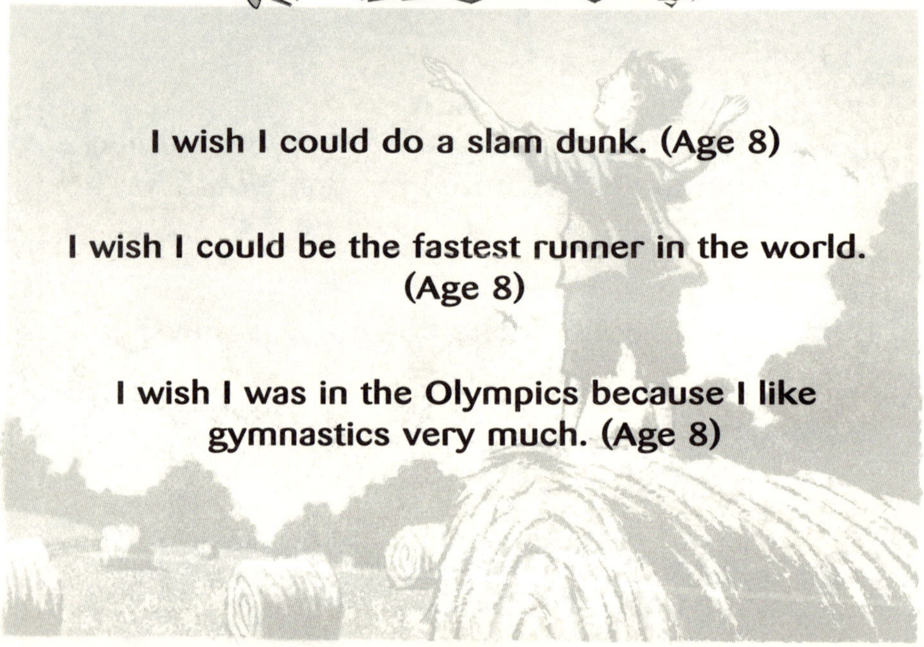

I wish I could do a slam dunk. (Age 8)

I wish I could be the fastest runner in the world. (Age 8)

I wish I was in the Olympics because I like gymnastics very much. (Age 8)

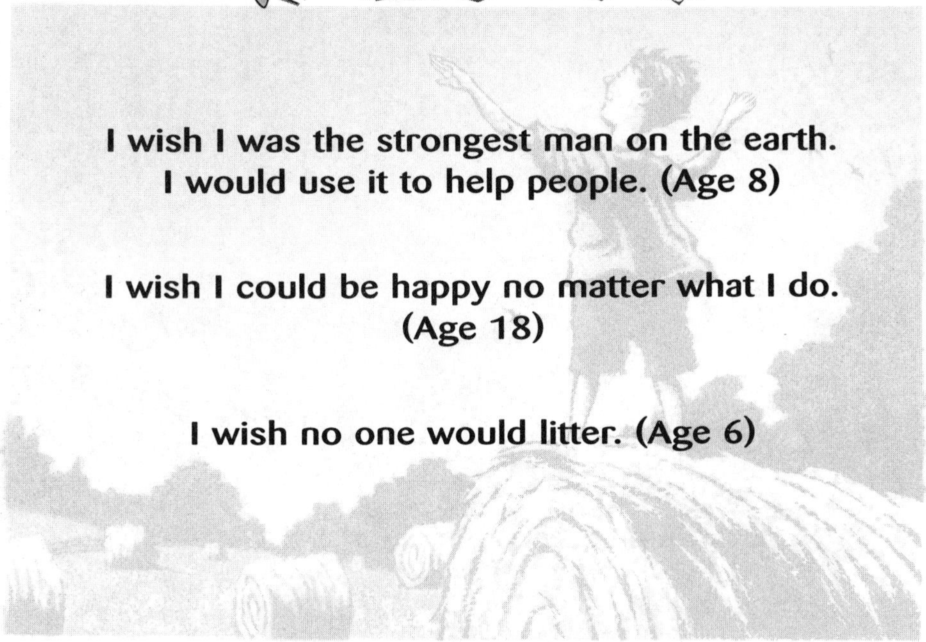

I wish I was the strongest man on the earth.
I would use it to help people. (Age 8)

I wish I could be happy no matter what I do.
(Age 18)

I wish no one would litter. (Age 6)

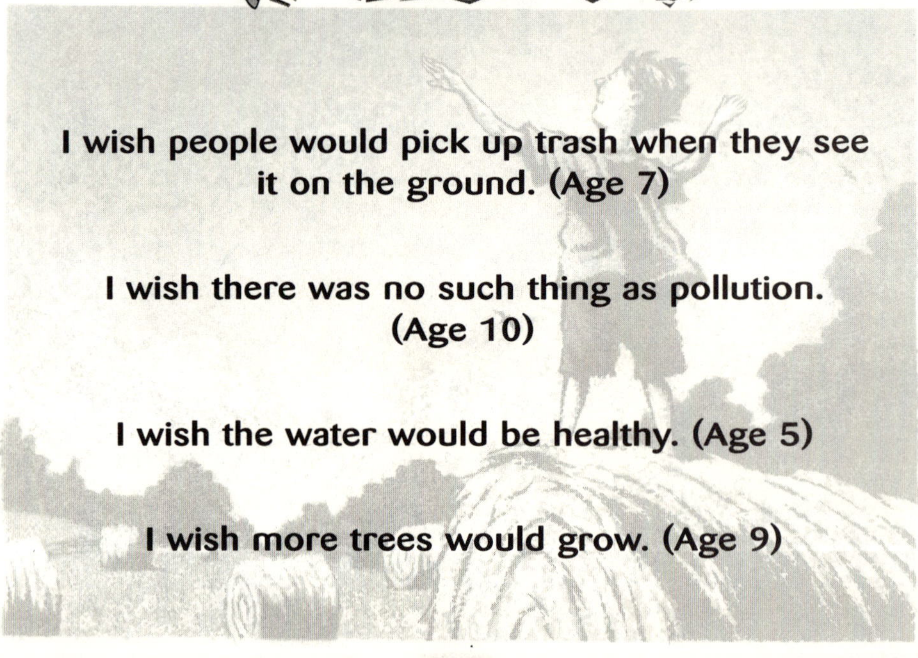

I wish people would pick up trash when they see it on the ground. (Age 7)

I wish there was no such thing as pollution. (Age 10)

I wish the water would be healthy. (Age 5)

I wish more trees would grow. (Age 9)

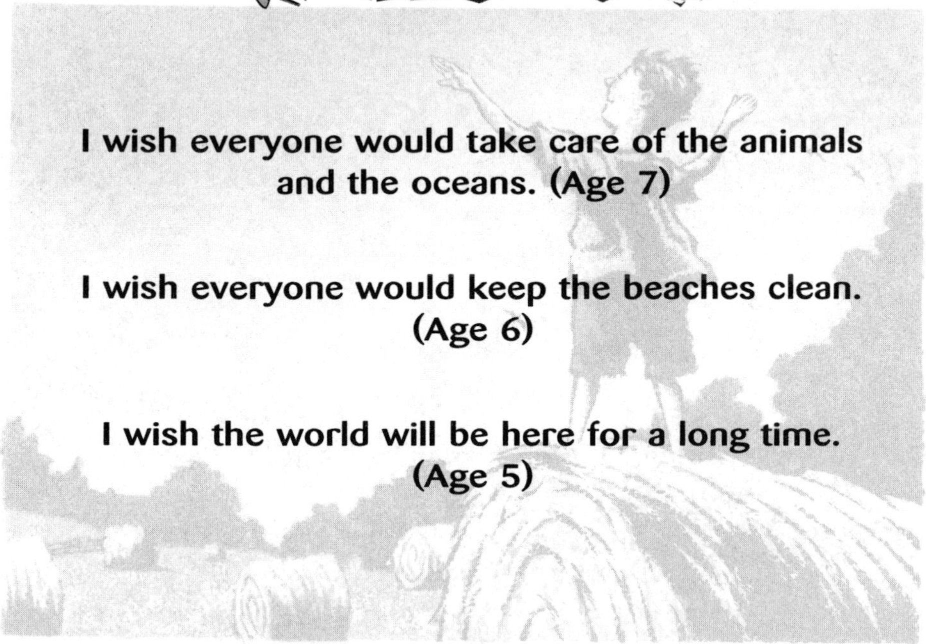

I wish everyone would take care of the animals and the oceans. (Age 7)

I wish everyone would keep the beaches clean. (Age 6)

I wish the world will be here for a long time. (Age 5)

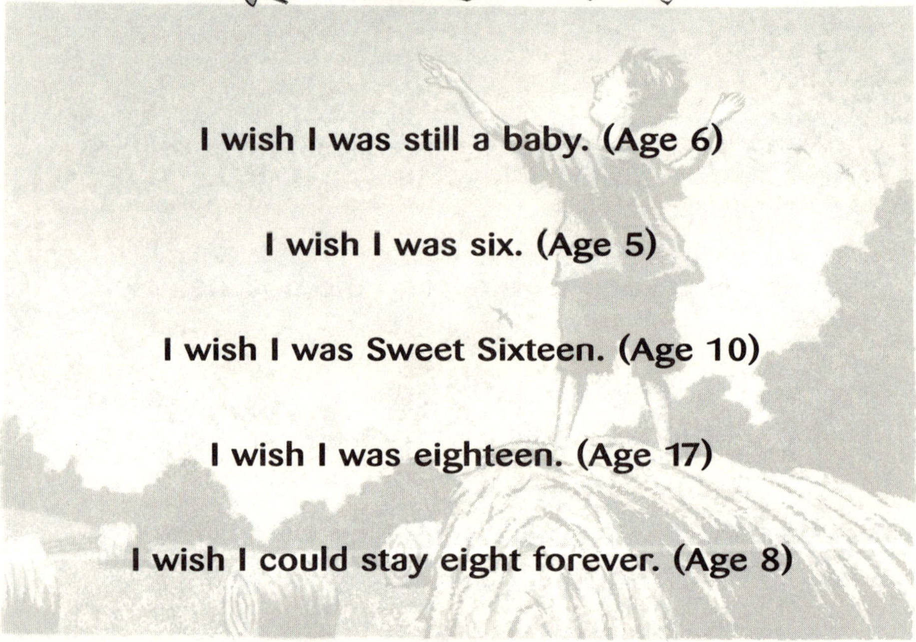

I wish I was still a baby. (Age 6)

I wish I was six. (Age 5)

I wish I was Sweet Sixteen. (Age 10)

I wish I was eighteen. (Age 17)

I wish I could stay eight forever. (Age 8)

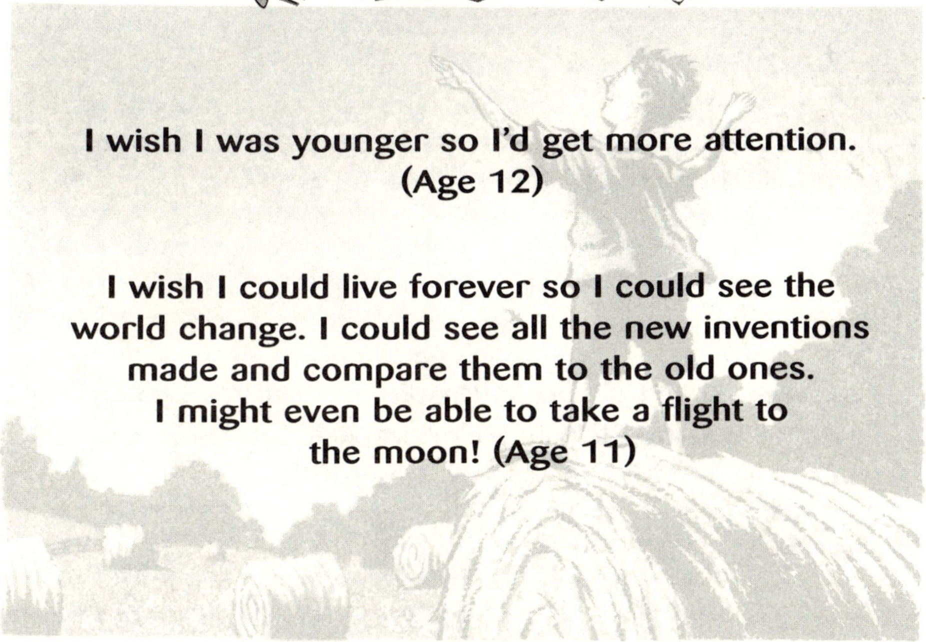

I wish I was younger so I'd get more attention.
(Age 12)

I wish I could live forever so I could see the world change. I could see all the new inventions made and compare them to the old ones. I might even be able to take a flight to the moon! (Age 11)

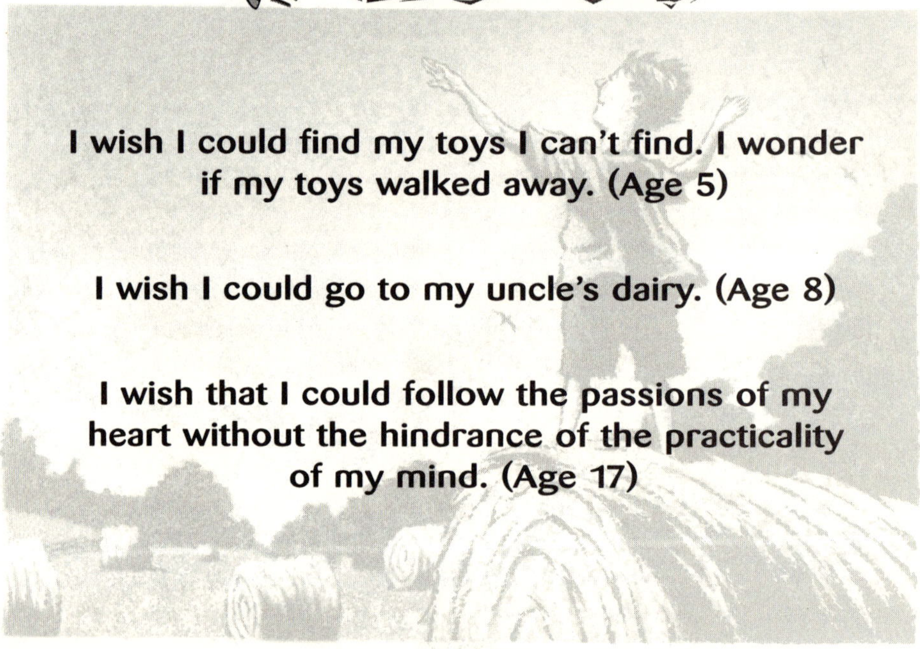

I wish I could find my toys I can't find. I wonder if my toys walked away. (Age 5)

I wish I could go to my uncle's dairy. (Age 8)

I wish that I could follow the passions of my heart without the hindrance of the practicality of my mind. (Age 17)

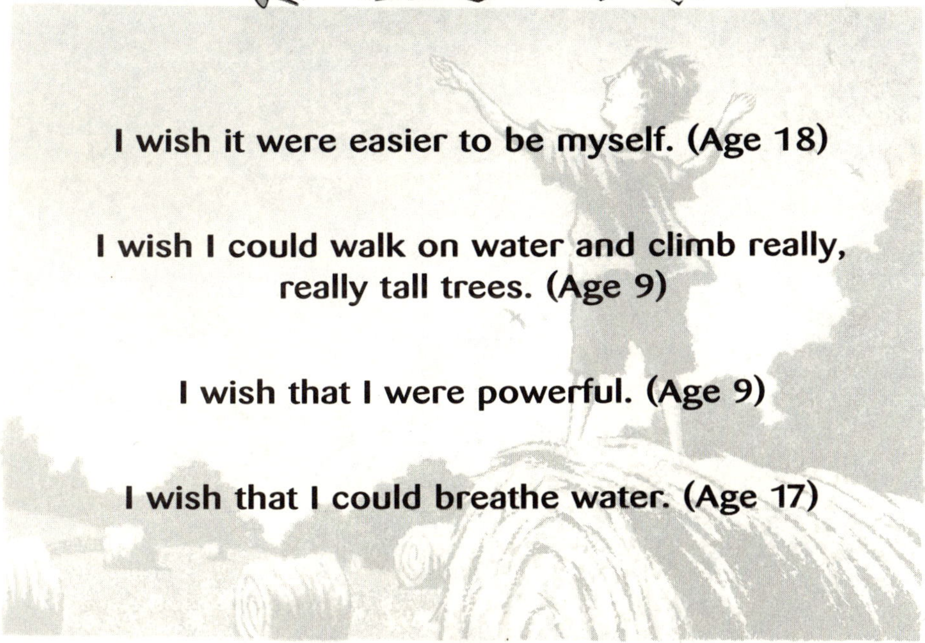

I wish it were easier to be myself. (Age 18)

I wish I could walk on water and climb really, really tall trees. (Age 9)

I wish that I were powerful. (Age 9)

I wish that I could breathe water. (Age 17)

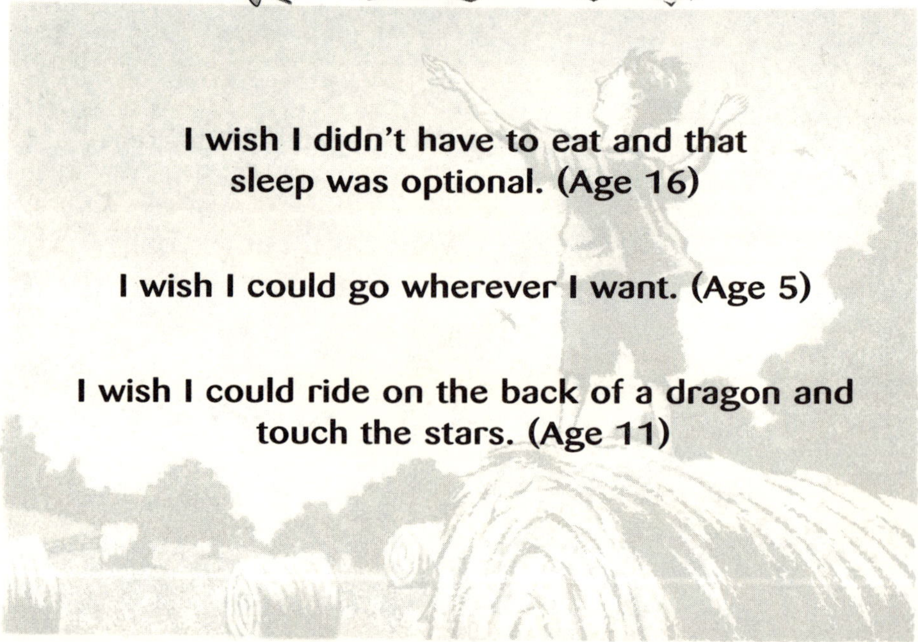

I wish I didn't have to eat and that sleep was optional. (Age 16)

I wish I could go wherever I want. (Age 5)

I wish I could ride on the back of a dragon and touch the stars. (Age 11)

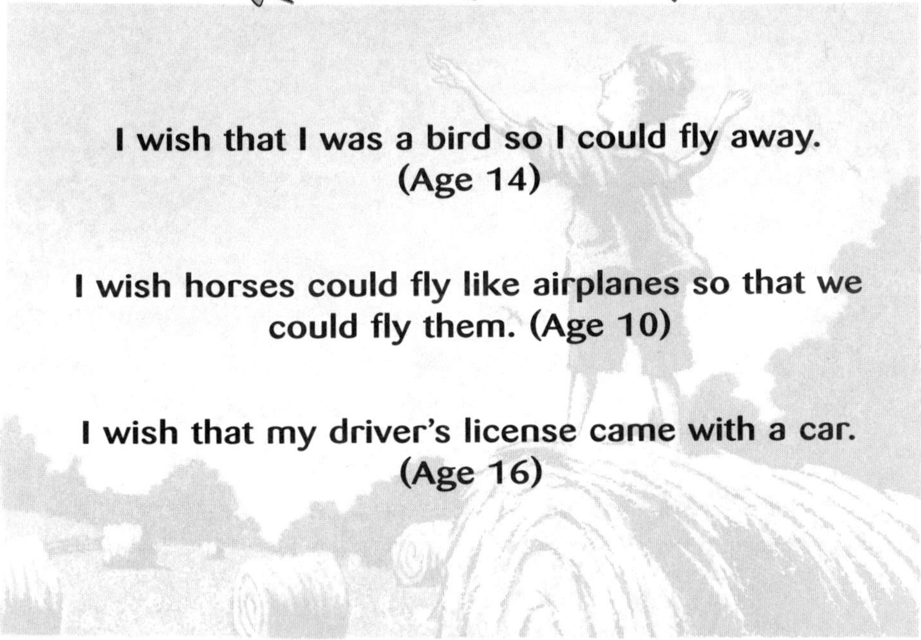

I wish that I was a bird so I could fly away. (Age 14)

I wish horses could fly like airplanes so that we could fly them. (Age 10)

I wish that my driver's license came with a car. (Age 16)

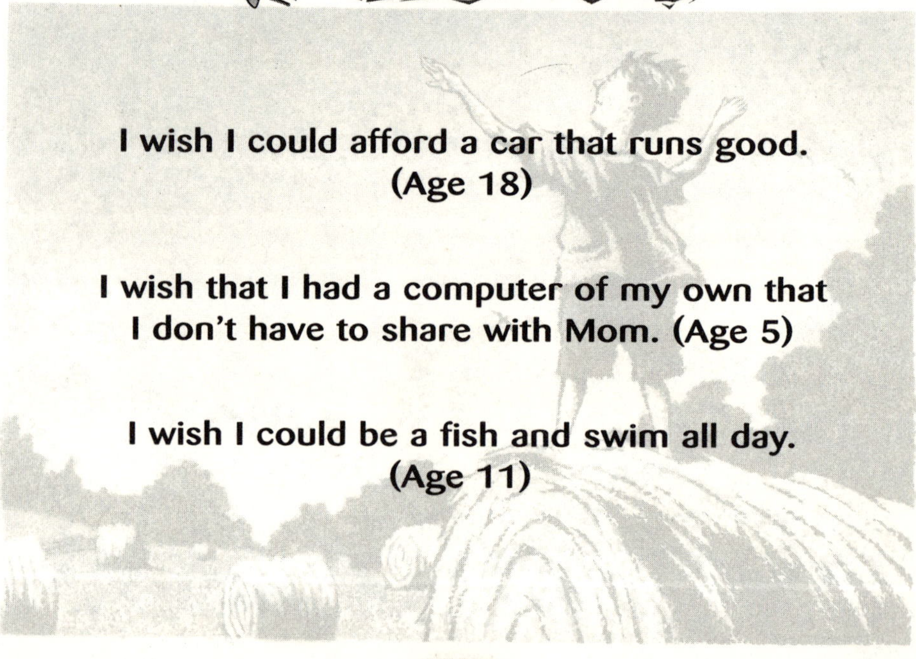

I wish I could afford a car that runs good. (Age 18)

I wish that I had a computer of my own that I don't have to share with Mom. (Age 5)

I wish I could be a fish and swim all day. (Age 11)

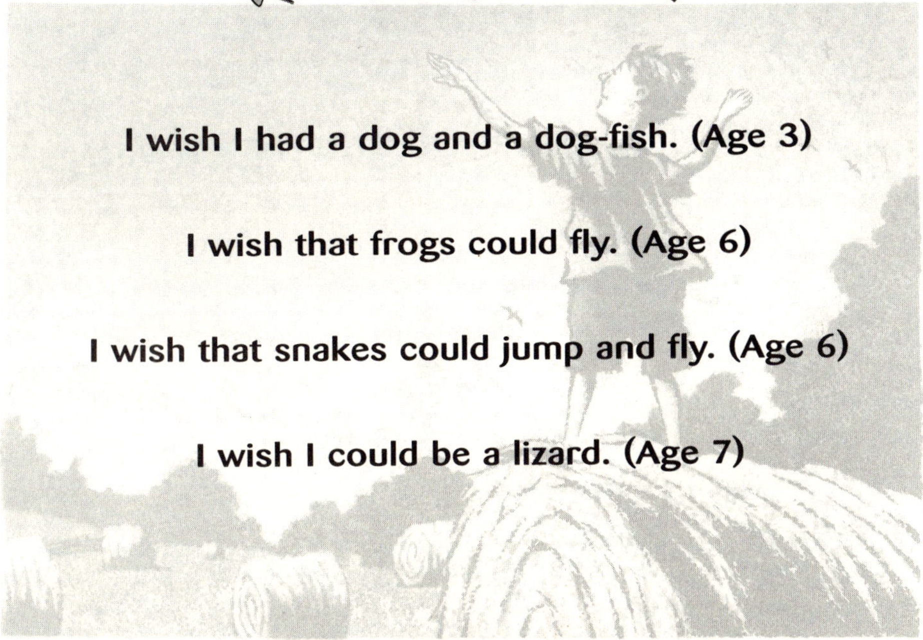

I wish I had a dog and a dog-fish. (Age 3)

I wish that frogs could fly. (Age 6)

I wish that snakes could jump and fly. (Age 6)

I wish I could be a lizard. (Age 7)

I wish I had a zebra to put in a cage. (Age 4)

I wish I could live on a farm and own lots of animals. (Age 15)

I wish my cat didn't die. (Age 5)

I wish I will always have pets. (Age 5)

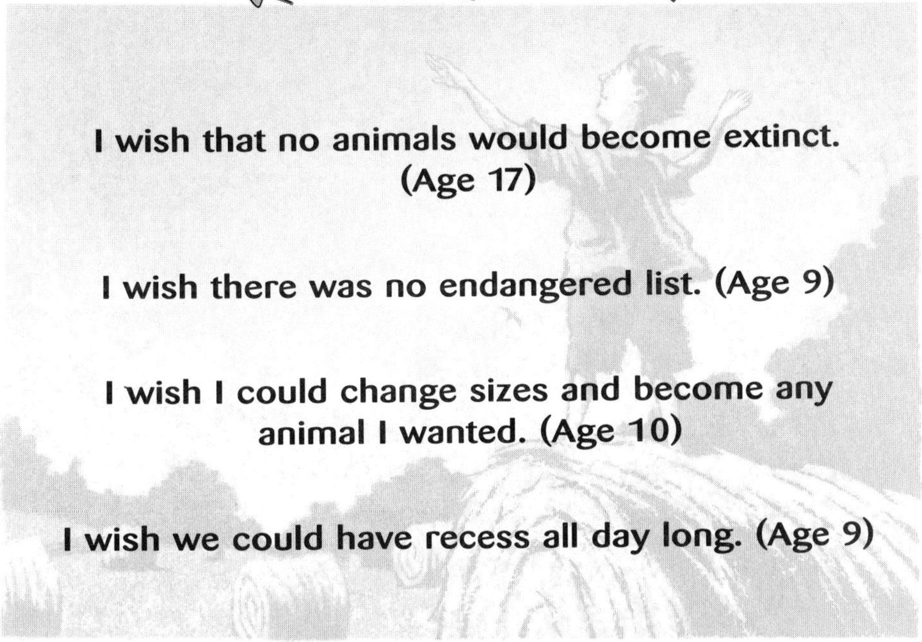

I wish that no animals would become extinct. (Age 17)

I wish there was no endangered list. (Age 9)

I wish I could change sizes and become any animal I wanted. (Age 10)

I wish we could have recess all day long. (Age 9)

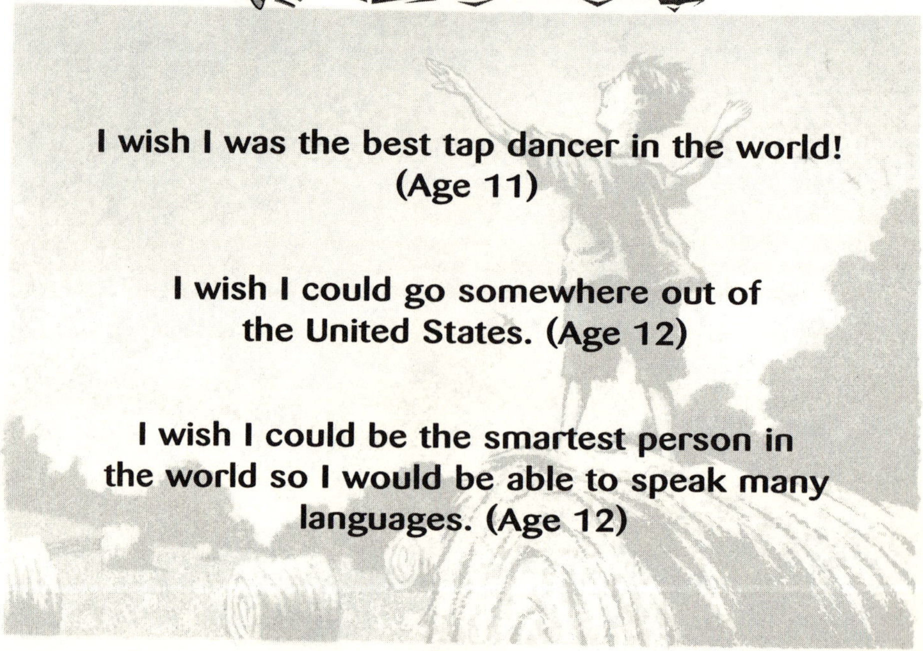

I wish I was the best tap dancer in the world! (Age 11)

I wish I could go somewhere out of the United States. (Age 12)

I wish I could be the smartest person in the world so I would be able to speak many languages. (Age 12)

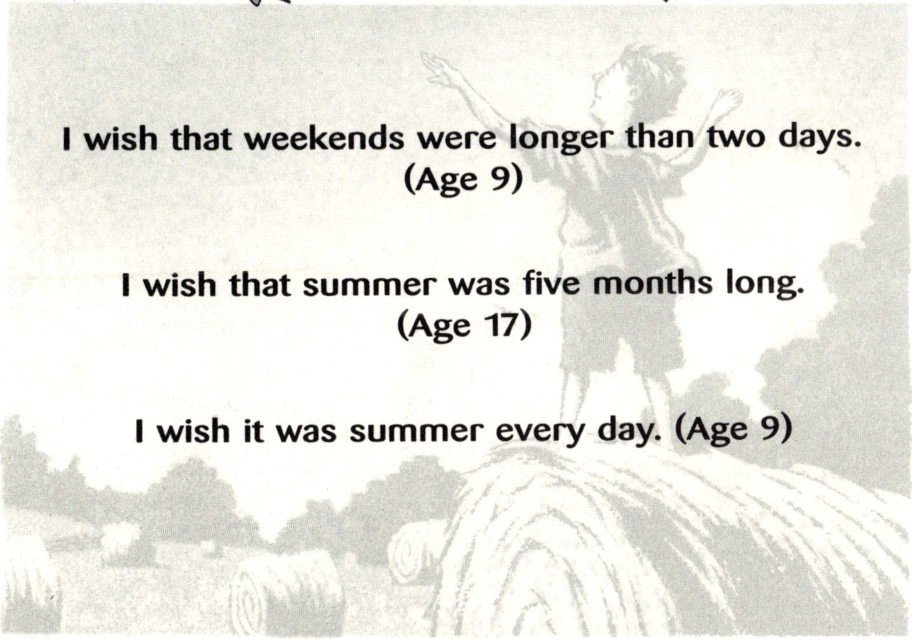

I wish that weekends were longer than two days. (Age 9)

I wish that summer was five months long. (Age 17)

I wish it was summer every day. (Age 9)

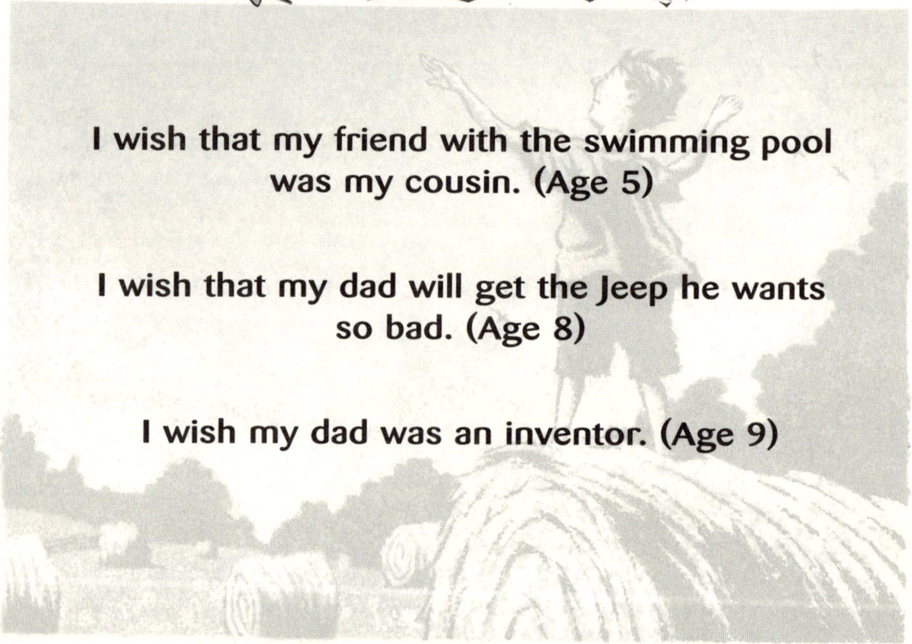

I wish that my friend with the swimming pool was my cousin. (Age 5)

I wish that my dad will get the Jeep he wants so bad. (Age 8)

I wish my dad was an inventor. (Age 9)

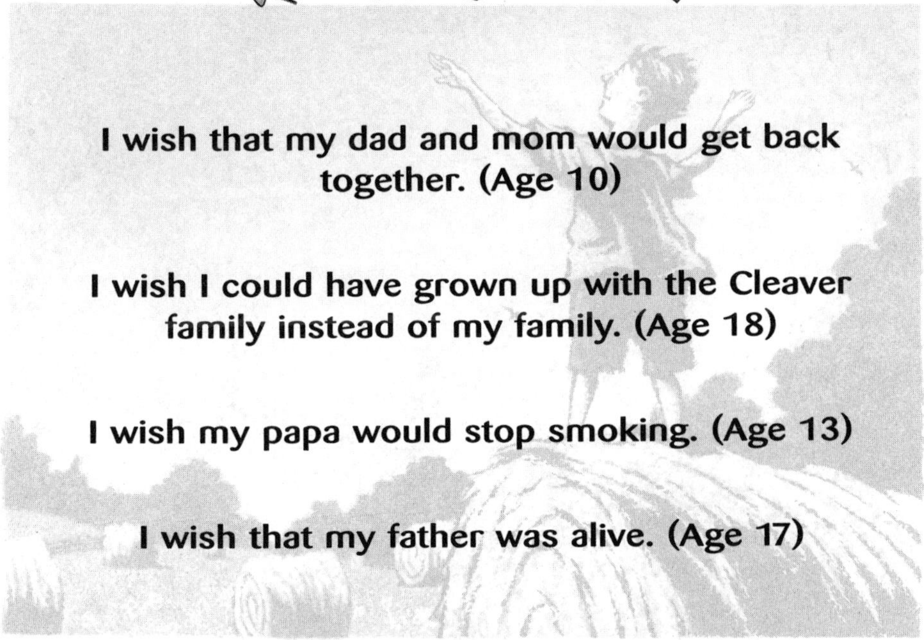

I wish that my dad and mom would get back together. (Age 10)

I wish I could have grown up with the Cleaver family instead of my family. (Age 18)

I wish my papa would stop smoking. (Age 13)

I wish that my father was alive. (Age 17)

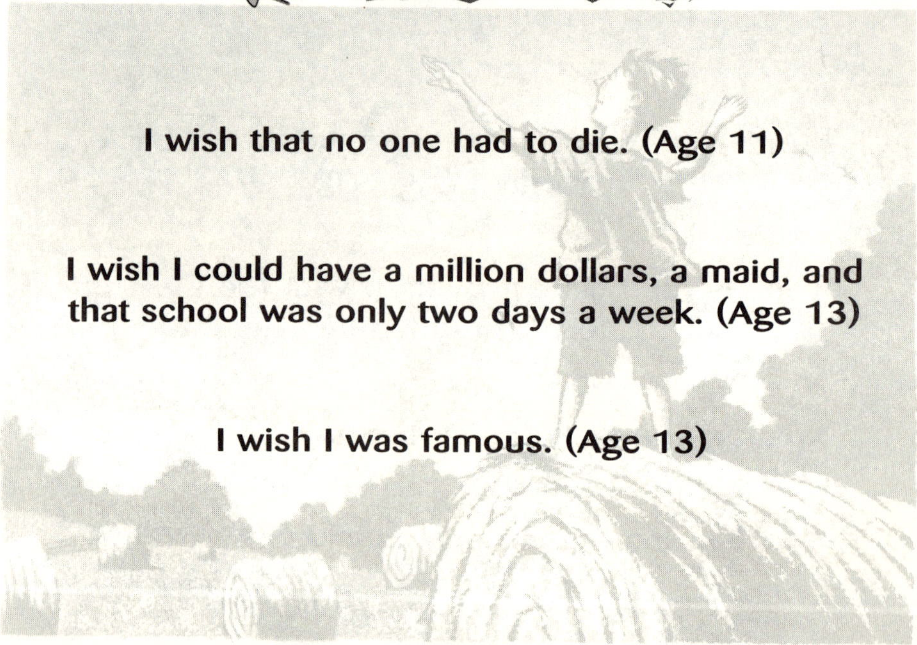

I wish that no one had to die. (Age 11)

I wish I could have a million dollars, a maid, and that school was only two days a week. (Age 13)

I wish I was famous. (Age 13)

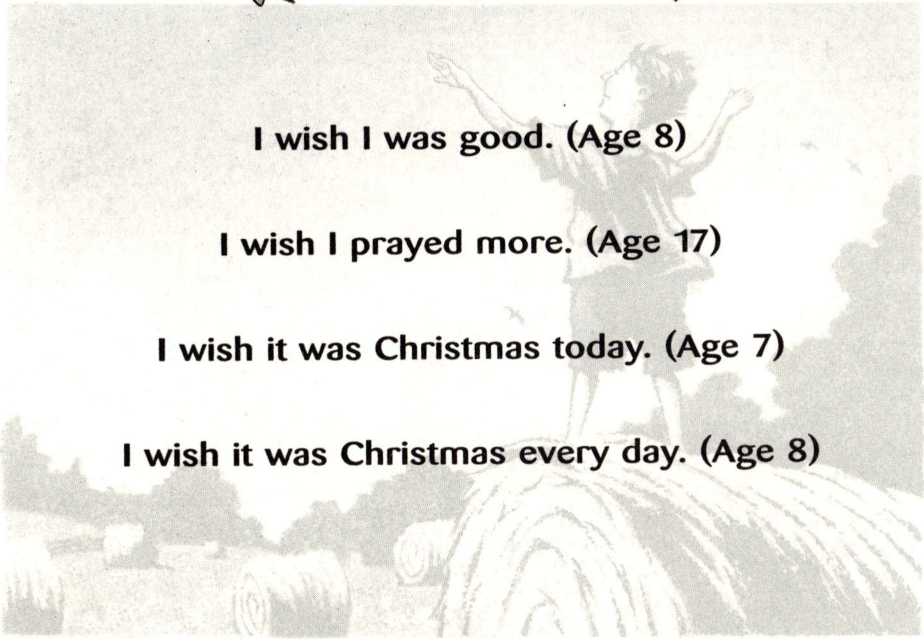

I wish I was good. (Age 8)

I wish I prayed more. (Age 17)

I wish it was Christmas today. (Age 7)

I wish it was Christmas every day. (Age 8)

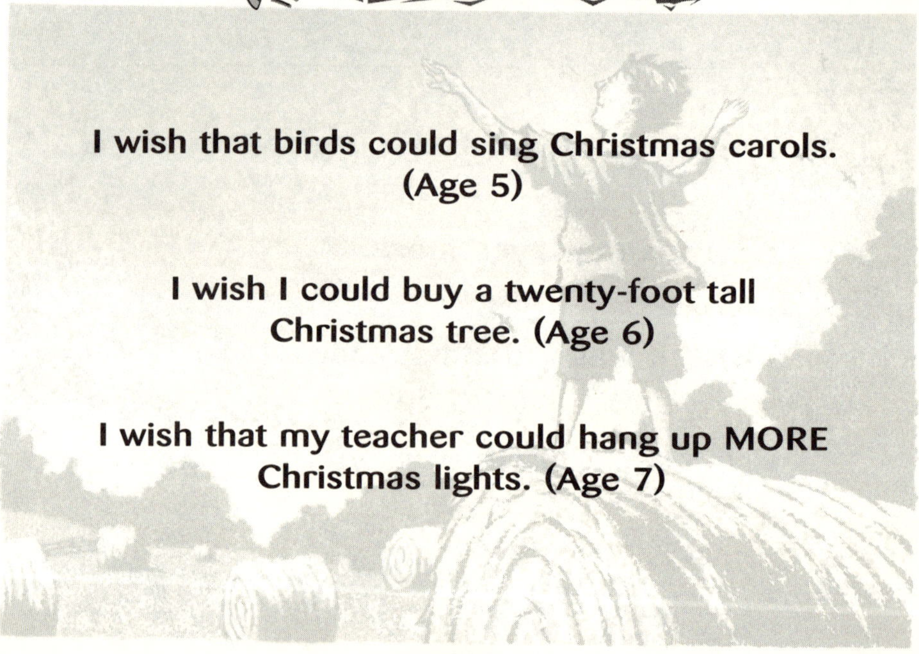

I wish that birds could sing Christmas carols. (Age 5)

I wish I could buy a twenty-foot tall Christmas tree. (Age 6)

I wish that my teacher could hang up MORE Christmas lights. (Age 7)

I wish that I liked pumpkin pie. (Age 5)

I wish nobody was allowed to yell and everybody spoke in quiet voices. (Age 16)

I wish that everybody had someone to talk to. (Age 11)

I wish I had a Barney birthday hat. (Age 2)

I wish I had a gum machine. (Age 3)

I wish I had a beeper and cell phone. (Age 8)

I wish I could own a theme park so I could invite all my friends to it. (Age 11)

I wish for new shoes. (Age 6)

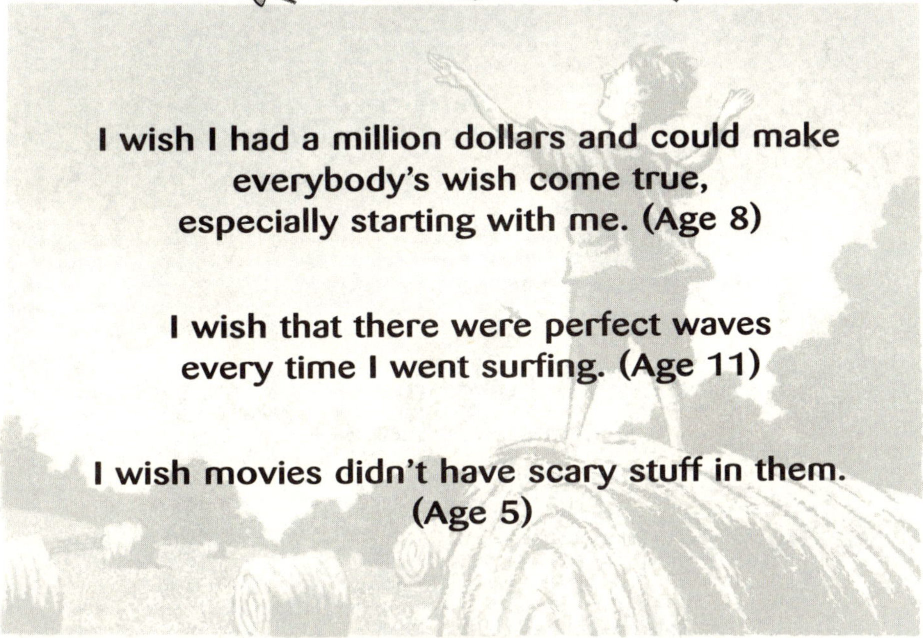

I wish I had a million dollars and could make everybody's wish come true, especially starting with me. (Age 8)

I wish that there were perfect waves every time I went surfing. (Age 11)

I wish movies didn't have scary stuff in them. (Age 5)

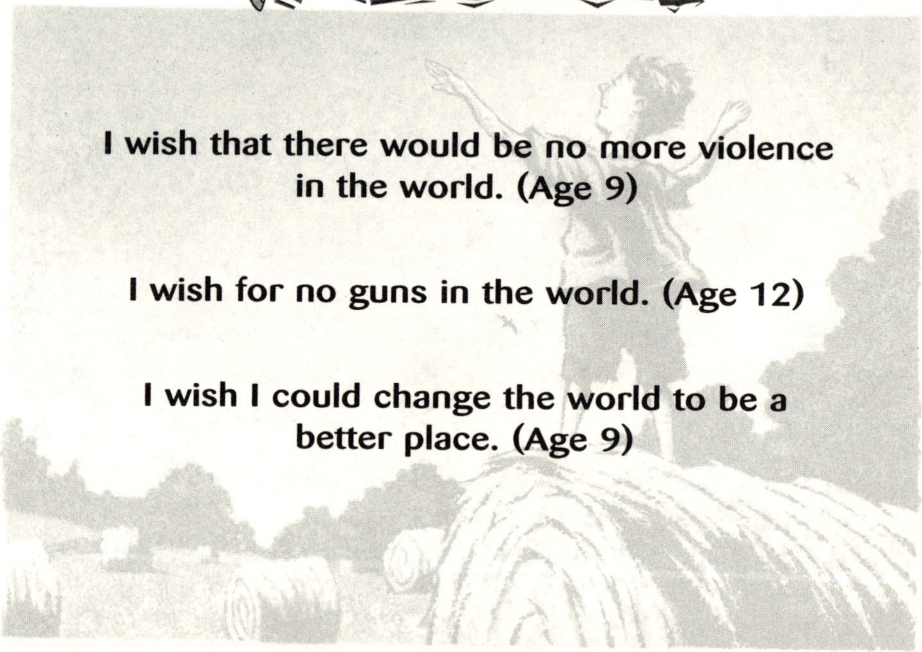

I wish that there would be no more violence in the world. (Age 9)

I wish for no guns in the world. (Age 12)

I wish I could change the world to be a better place. (Age 9)

I wish I could go back in time and see my parents as children. (Age 18)

I wish I could own a time machine so I could travel to the dinosaurs, see the Civil War, and ancient India. Plus, I could see the future, like 2098. (Age 11)

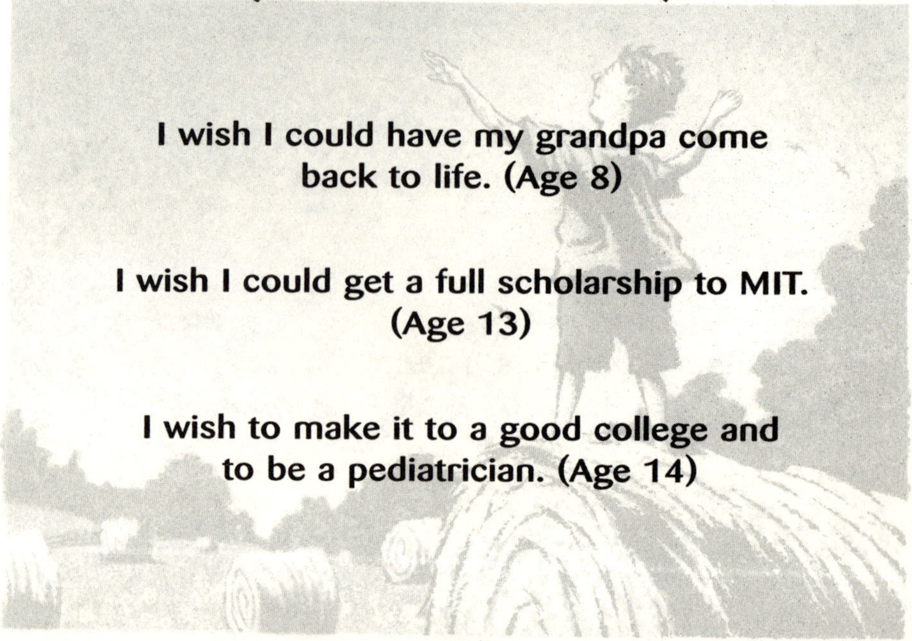

I wish I could have my grandpa come back to life. (Age 8)

I wish I could get a full scholarship to MIT. (Age 13)

I wish to make it to a good college and to be a pediatrician. (Age 14)

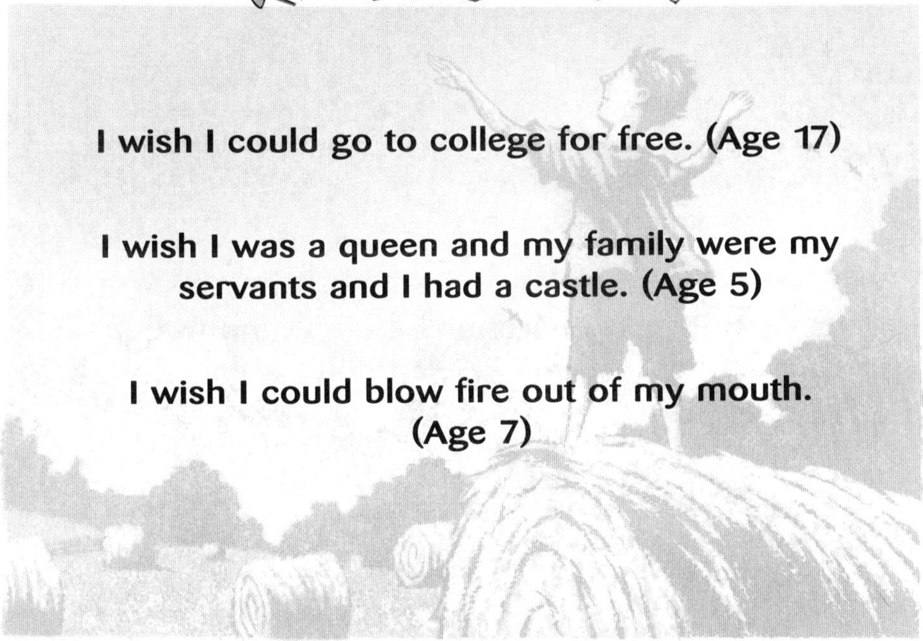

I wish I could go to college for free. (Age 17)

I wish I was a queen and my family were my servants and I had a castle. (Age 5)

I wish I could blow fire out of my mouth. (Age 7)

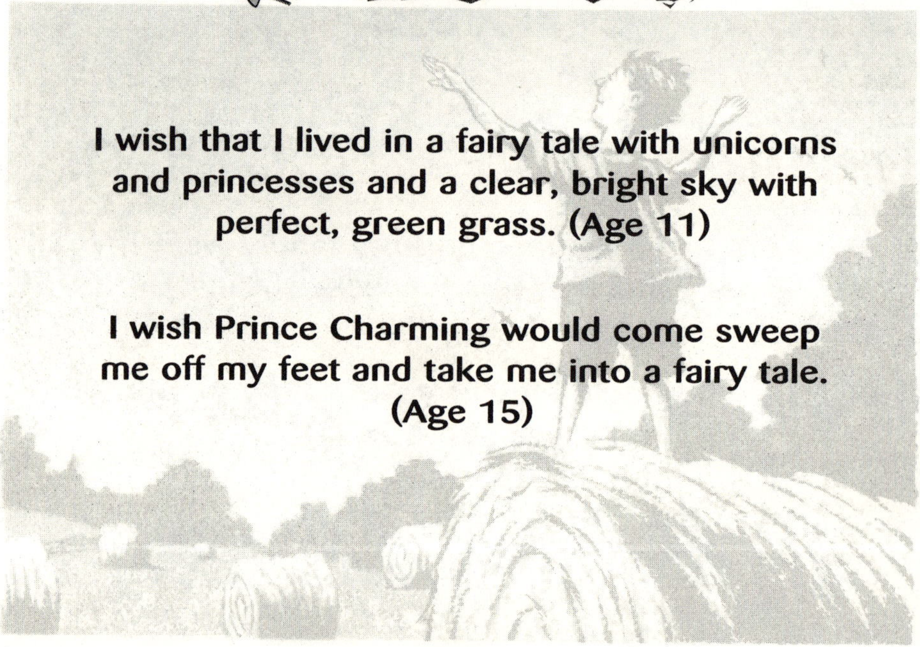

I wish that I lived in a fairy tale with unicorns and princesses and a clear, bright sky with perfect, green grass. (Age 11)

I wish Prince Charming would come sweep me off my feet and take me into a fairy tale. (Age 15)

I wish that if you said that you just wanted your friends in your class it would happen. (Age 10)

I wish friends really were always there when you need them. (Age 15)

I wish I could meet every baseball player. (Age 11)

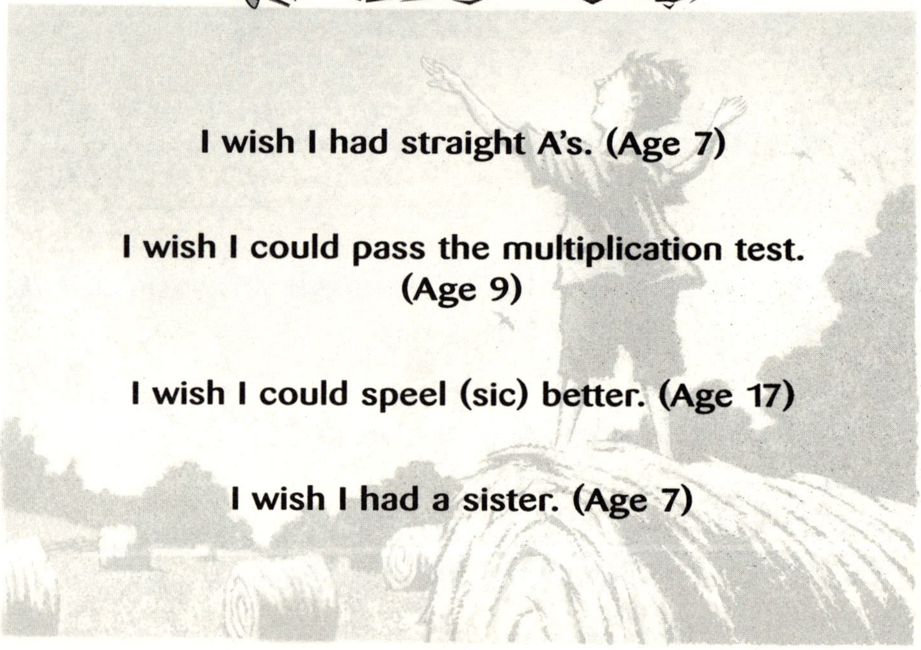

I wish I had straight A's. (Age 7)

I wish I could pass the multiplication test. (Age 9)

I wish I could speel (sic) better. (Age 17)

I wish I had a sister. (Age 7)

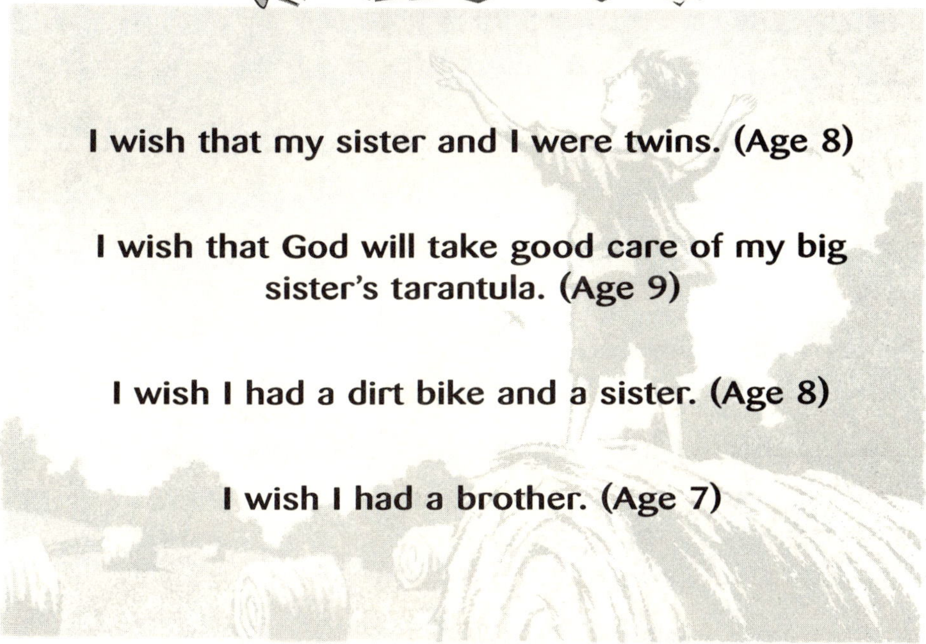

I wish that my sister and I were twins. (Age 8)

I wish that God will take good care of my big sister's tarantula. (Age 9)

I wish I had a dirt bike and a sister. (Age 8)

I wish I had a brother. (Age 7)

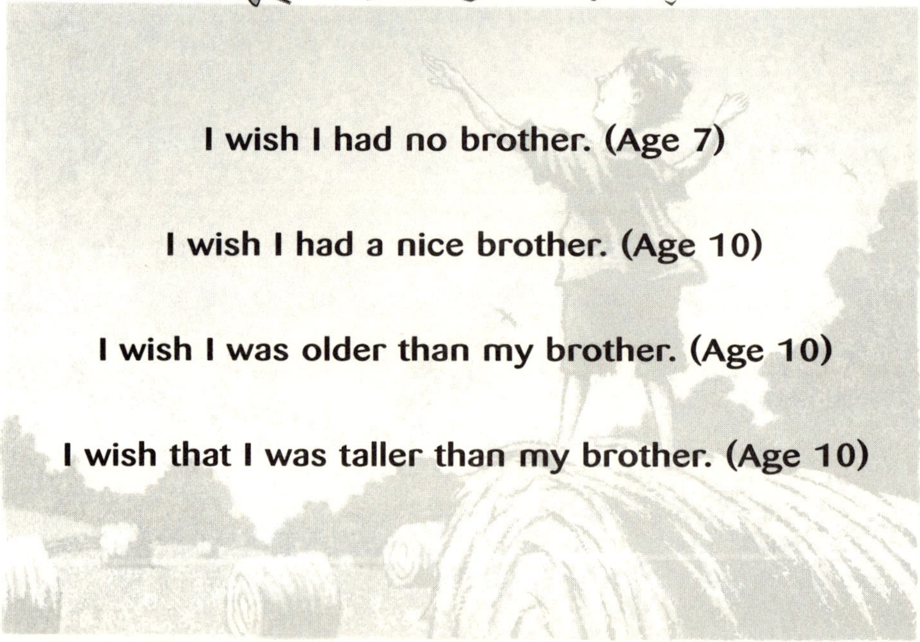

I wish I had no brother. (Age 7)

I wish I had a nice brother. (Age 10)

I wish I was older than my brother. (Age 10)

I wish that I was taller than my brother. (Age 10)

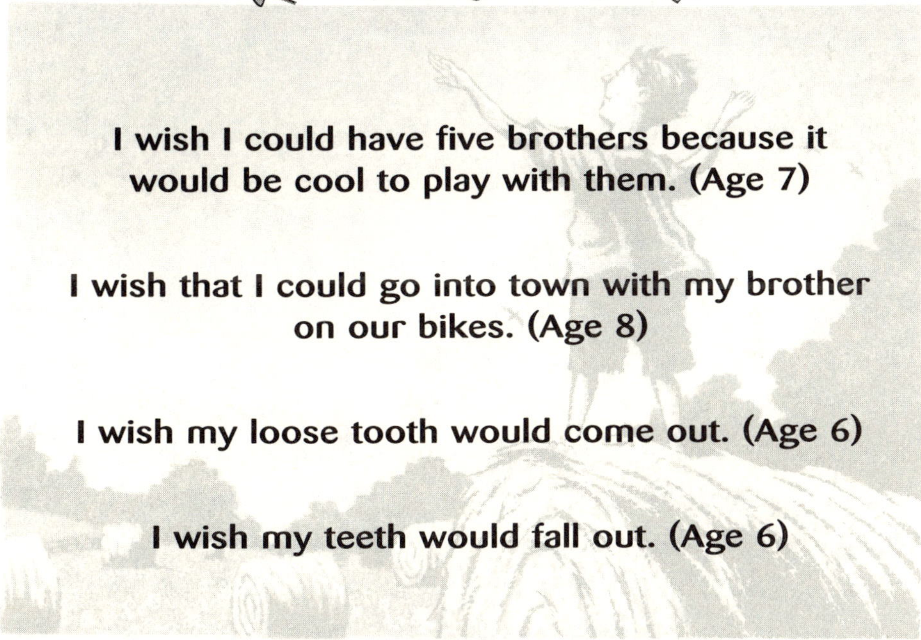

I wish I could have five brothers because it would be cool to play with them. (Age 7)

I wish that I could go into town with my brother on our bikes. (Age 8)

I wish my loose tooth would come out. (Age 6)

I wish my teeth would fall out. (Age 6)

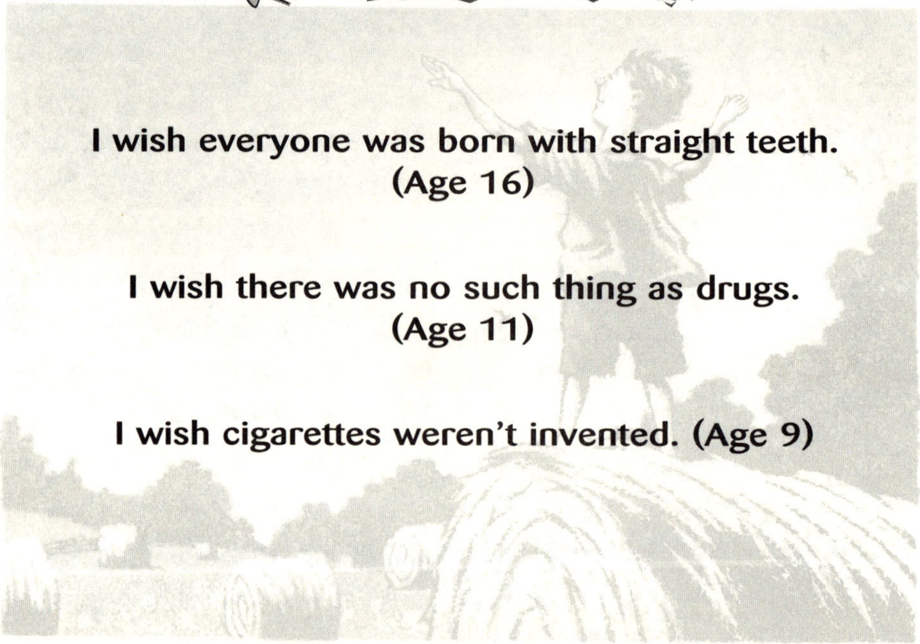

I wish everyone was born with straight teeth.
(Age 16)

I wish there was no such thing as drugs.
(Age 11)

I wish cigarettes weren't invented. (Age 9)

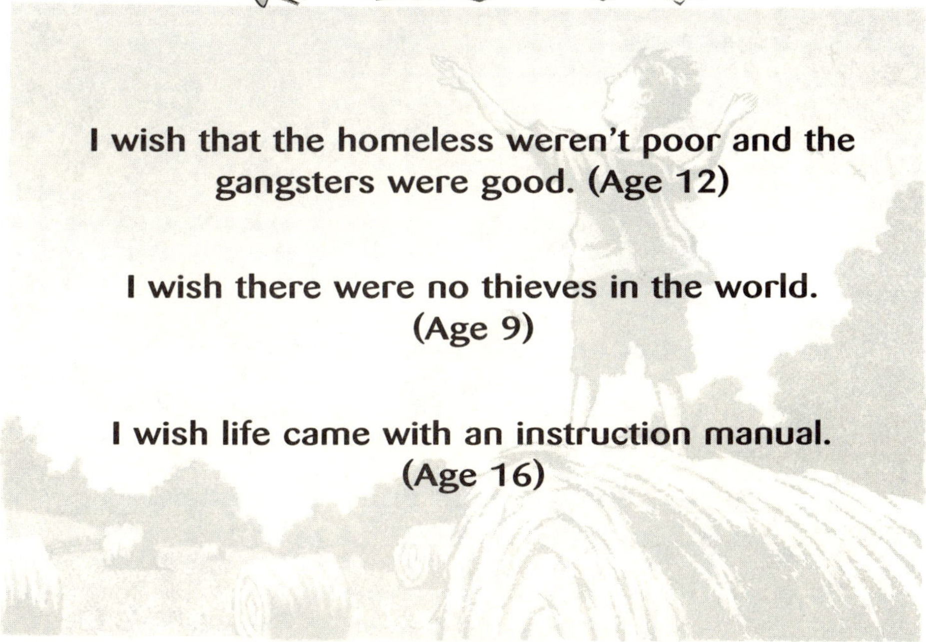

I wish that the homeless weren't poor and the gangsters were good. (Age 12)

I wish there were no thieves in the world. (Age 9)

I wish life came with an instruction manual. (Age 16)

I wish to be a cop. (Age 8)

I wish I was a star. (Age 12)

I wish I could be a famous singer and live in Paris. (Age 13)

I wish I could sing good enough to be on Broadway. (Age 18)

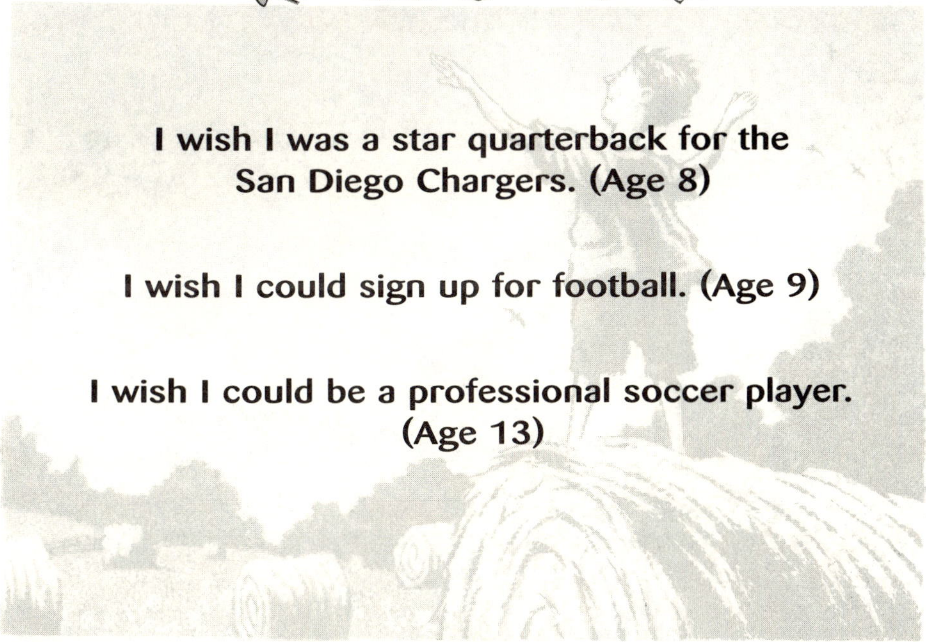

I wish I was a star quarterback for the San Diego Chargers. (Age 8)

I wish I could sign up for football. (Age 9)

I wish I could be a professional soccer player. (Age 13)

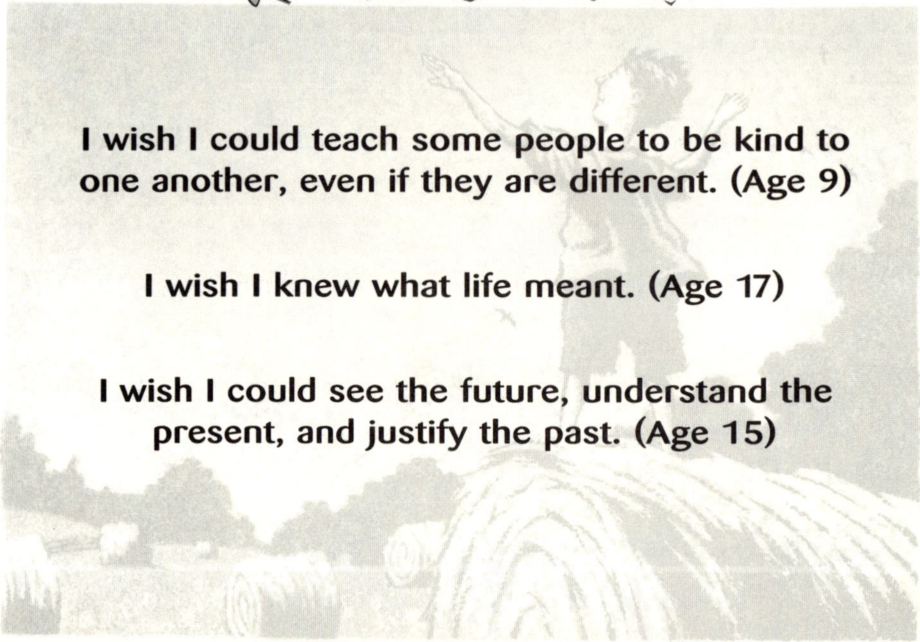

I wish I could teach some people to be kind to one another, even if they are different. (Age 9)

I wish I knew what life meant. (Age 17)

I wish I could see the future, understand the present, and justify the past. (Age 15)

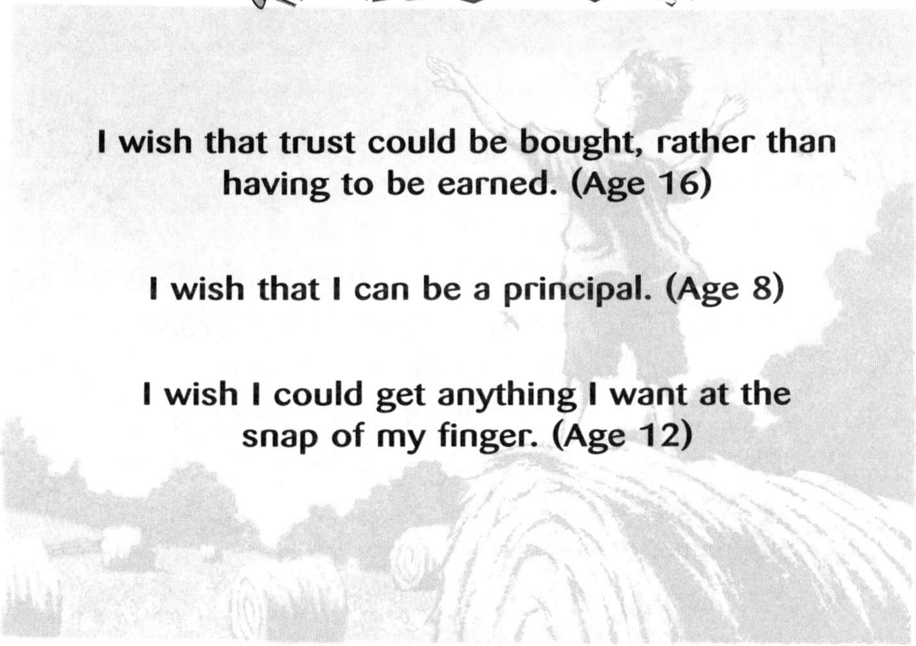

I wish that trust could be bought, rather than having to be earned. (Age 16)

I wish that I can be a principal. (Age 8)

I wish I could get anything I want at the snap of my finger. (Age 12)

I wish I had a robot to do my homework every day. (Age 9)

I wish I had a robot that would clean my room. It would be called Robo-Clean. (Age 8)

I wish I always listened to my mommy the first time. (Age 5)

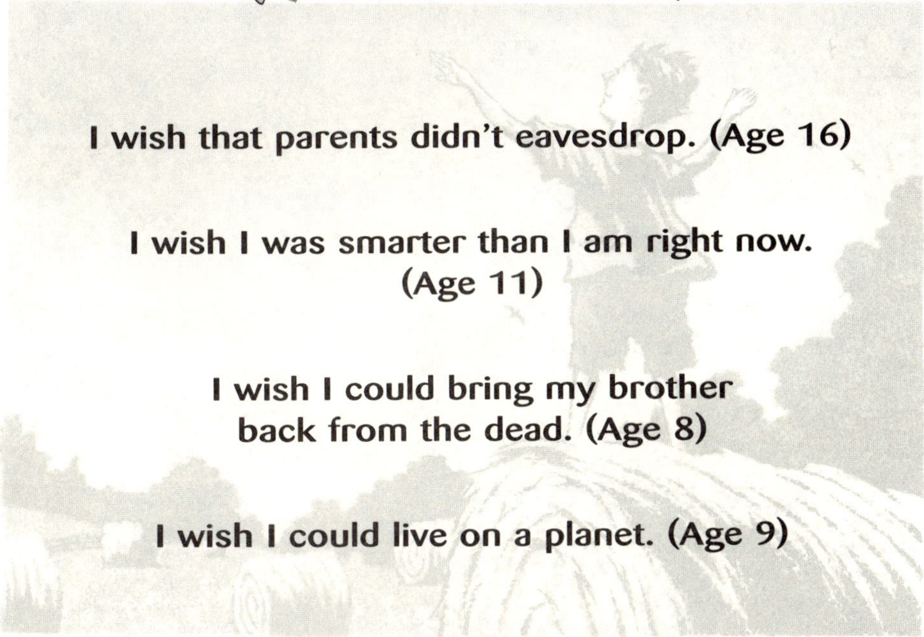

I wish that parents didn't eavesdrop. (Age 16)

I wish I was smarter than I am right now.
(Age 11)

I wish I could bring my brother
back from the dead. (Age 8)

I wish I could live on a planet. (Age 9)

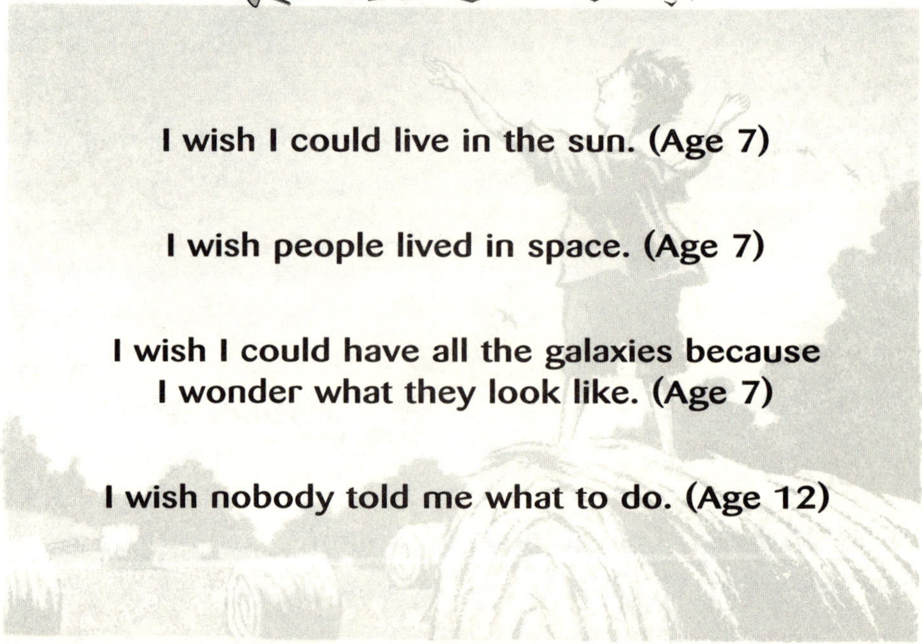

I wish I could live in the sun. (Age 7)

I wish people lived in space. (Age 7)

I wish I could have all the galaxies because
I wonder what they look like. (Age 7)

I wish nobody told me what to do. (Age 12)

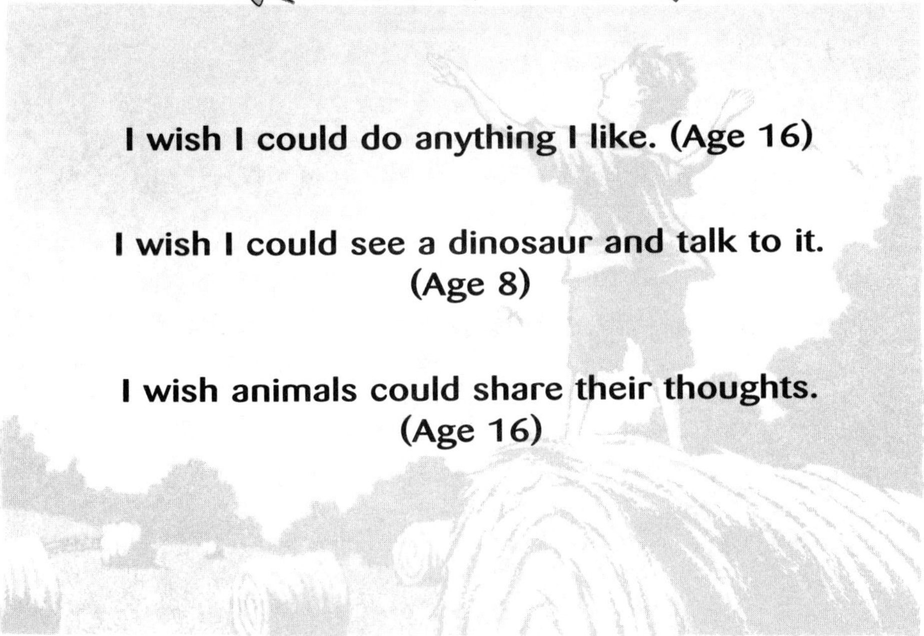

I wish I could do anything I like. (Age 16)

I wish I could see a dinosaur and talk to it. (Age 8)

I wish animals could share their thoughts. (Age 16)

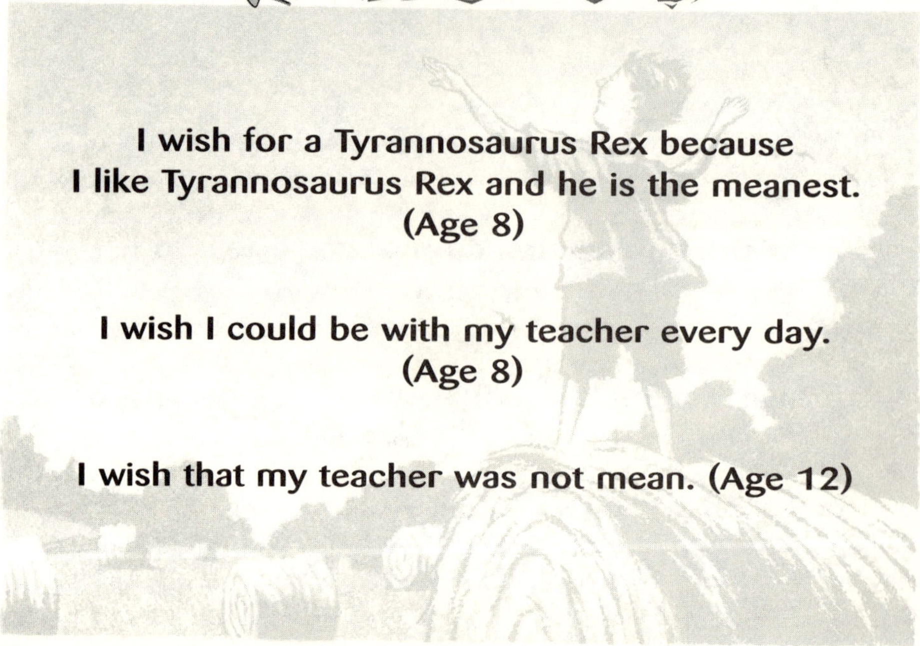

I wish for a Tyrannosaurus Rex because I like Tyrannosaurus Rex and he is the meanest.
(Age 8)

I wish I could be with my teacher every day.
(Age 8)

I wish that my teacher was not mean. (Age 12)

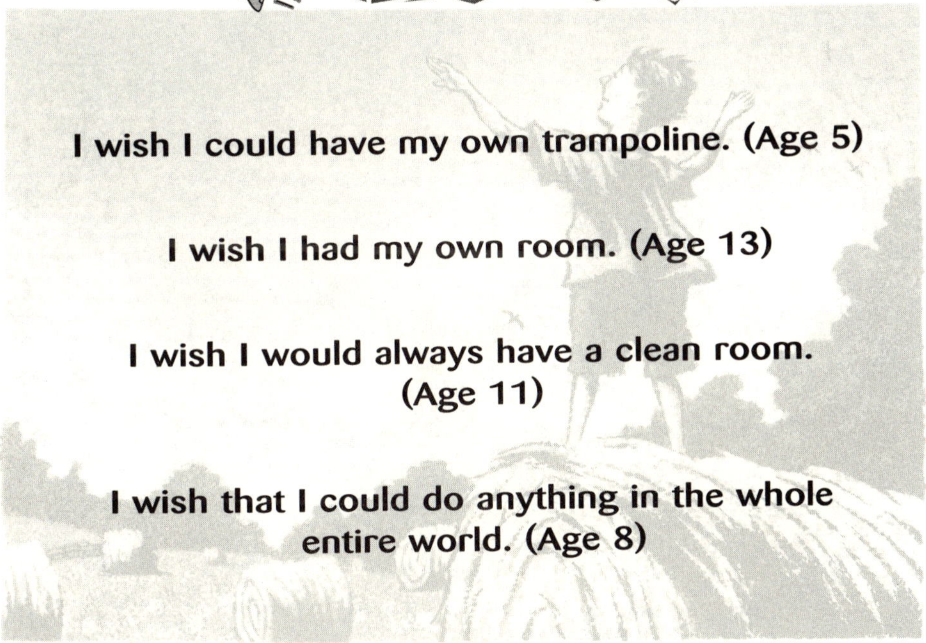

I wish I could have my own trampoline. (Age 5)

I wish I had my own room. (Age 13)

I wish I would always have a clean room. (Age 11)

I wish that I could do anything in the whole entire world. (Age 8)

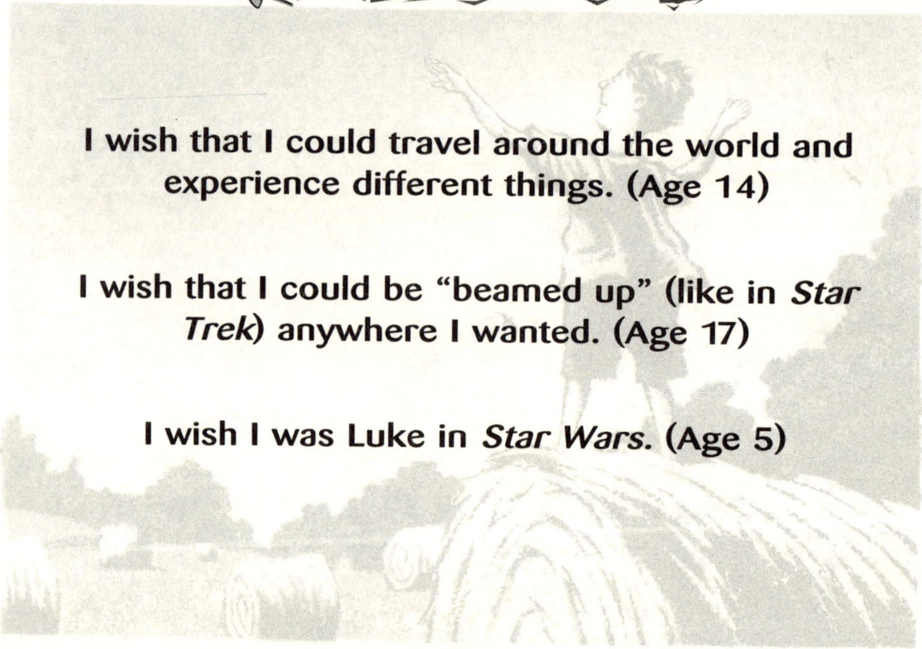

I wish that I could travel around the world and experience different things. (Age 14)

I wish that I could be "beamed up" (like in *Star Trek*) anywhere I wanted. (Age 17)

I wish I was Luke in *Star Wars.* (Age 5)

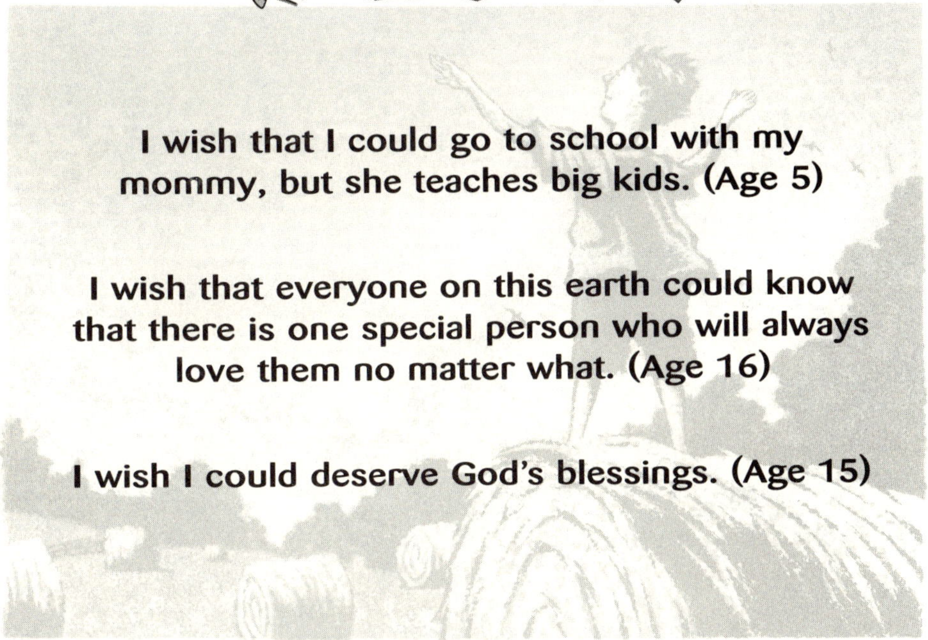

I wish that I could go to school with my mommy, but she teaches big kids. (Age 5)

I wish that everyone on this earth could know that there is one special person who will always love them no matter what. (Age 16)

I wish I could deserve God's blessings. (Age 15)

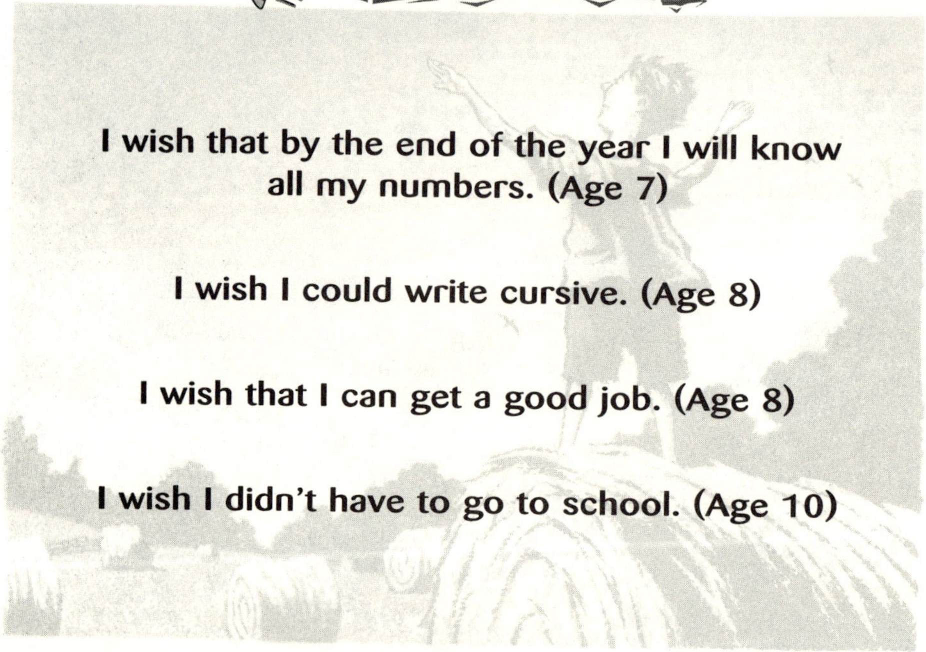

I wish that by the end of the year I will know all my numbers. (Age 7)

I wish I could write cursive. (Age 8)

I wish that I can get a good job. (Age 8)

I wish I didn't have to go to school. (Age 10)

I wish manners were non-existent. (Age 16)

I wish when I grow up I would have a girlfriend. (Age 5)

I wish a boy liked me. (Age 11)

I wish a broken heart was easier to mend. (Age 18)

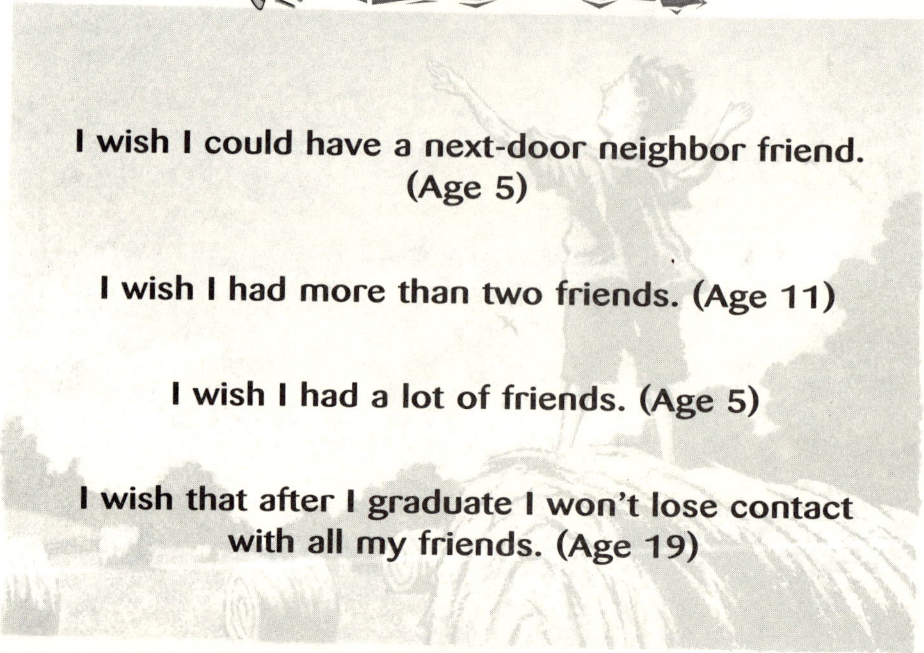

I wish I could have a next-door neighbor friend. (Age 5)

I wish I had more than two friends. (Age 11)

I wish I had a lot of friends. (Age 5)

I wish that after I graduate I won't lose contact with all my friends. (Age 19)

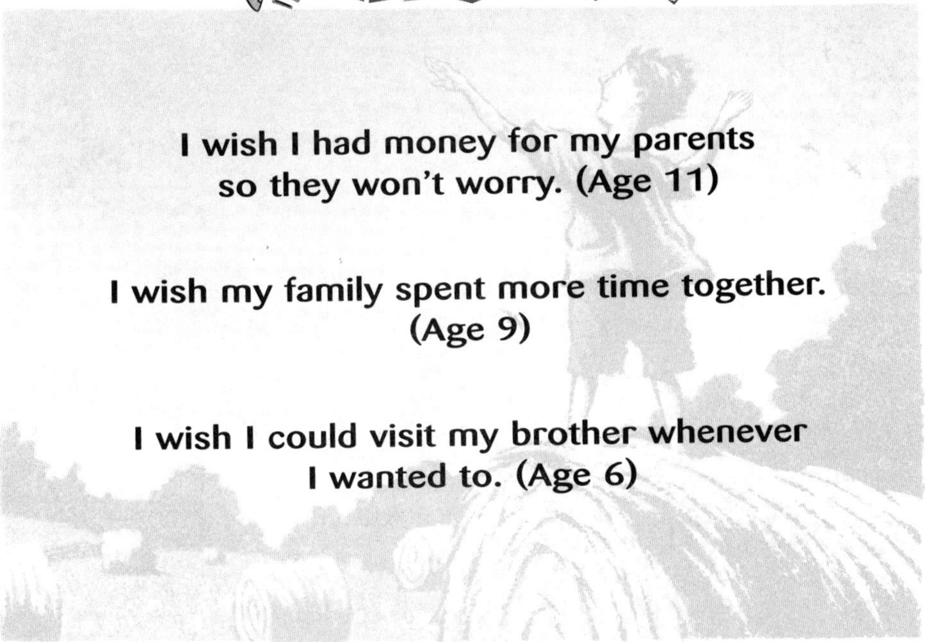

I wish I had money for my parents
so they won't worry. (Age 11)

I wish my family spent more time together.
(Age 9)

I wish I could visit my brother whenever
I wanted to. (Age 6)

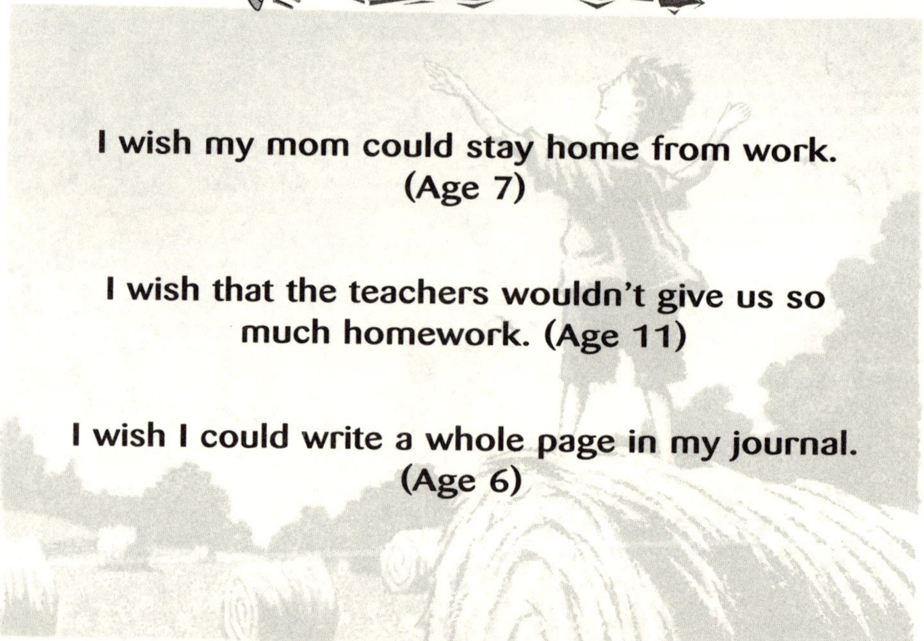

I wish my mom could stay home from work. (Age 7)

I wish that the teachers wouldn't give us so much homework. (Age 11)

I wish I could write a whole page in my journal. (Age 6)

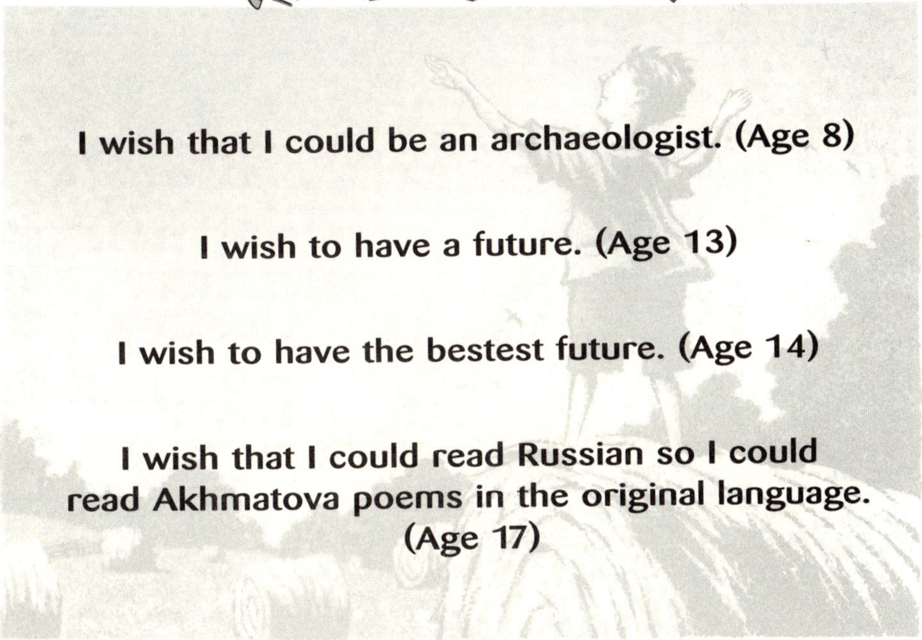

I wish that I could be an archaeologist. (Age 8)

I wish to have a future. (Age 13)

I wish to have the bestest future. (Age 14)

I wish that I could read Russian so I could read Akhmatova poems in the original language. (Age 17)

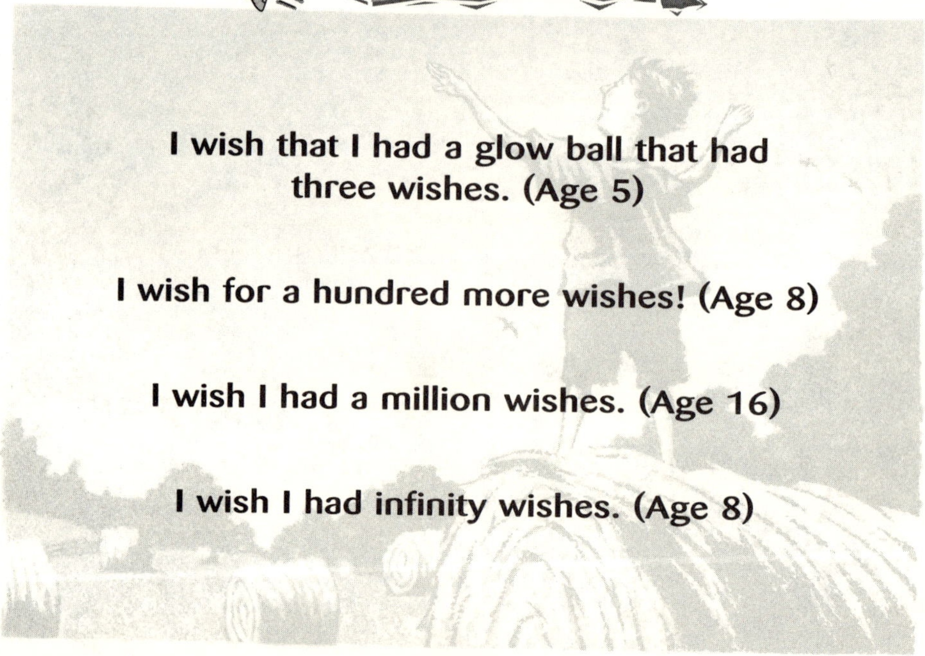

I wish that I had a glow ball that had three wishes. (Age 5)

I wish for a hundred more wishes! (Age 8)

I wish I had a million wishes. (Age 16)

I wish I had infinity wishes. (Age 8)

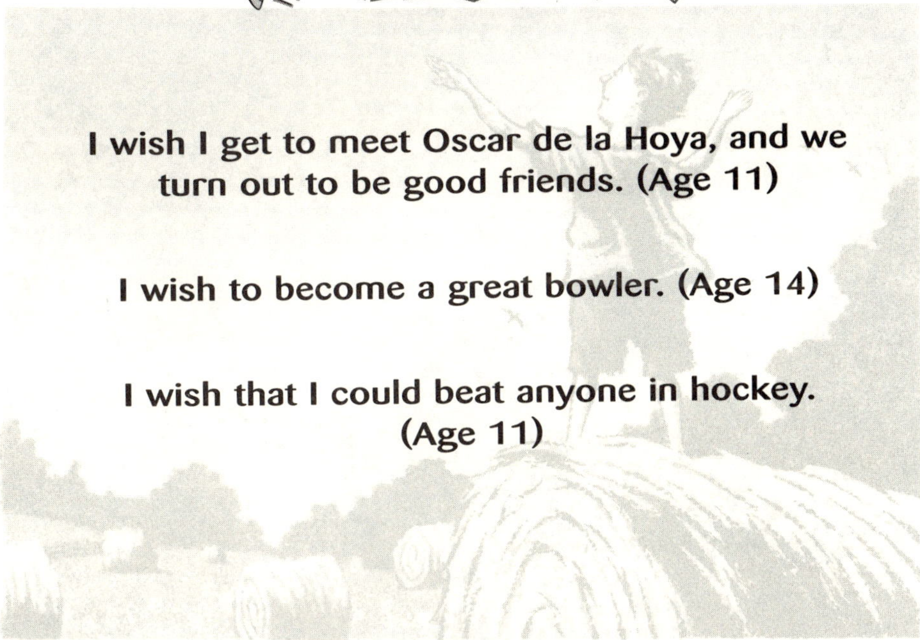

I wish I get to meet Oscar de la Hoya, and we turn out to be good friends. (Age 11)

I wish to become a great bowler. (Age 14)

I wish that I could beat anyone in hockey. (Age 11)

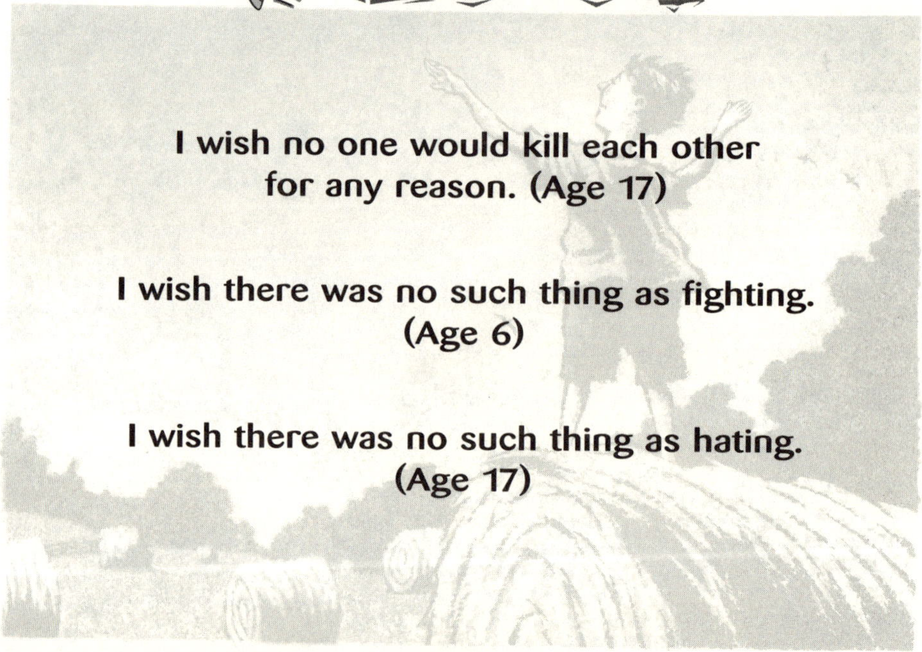

I wish no one would kill each other for any reason. (Age 17)

I wish there was no such thing as fighting. (Age 6)

I wish there was no such thing as hating. (Age 17)

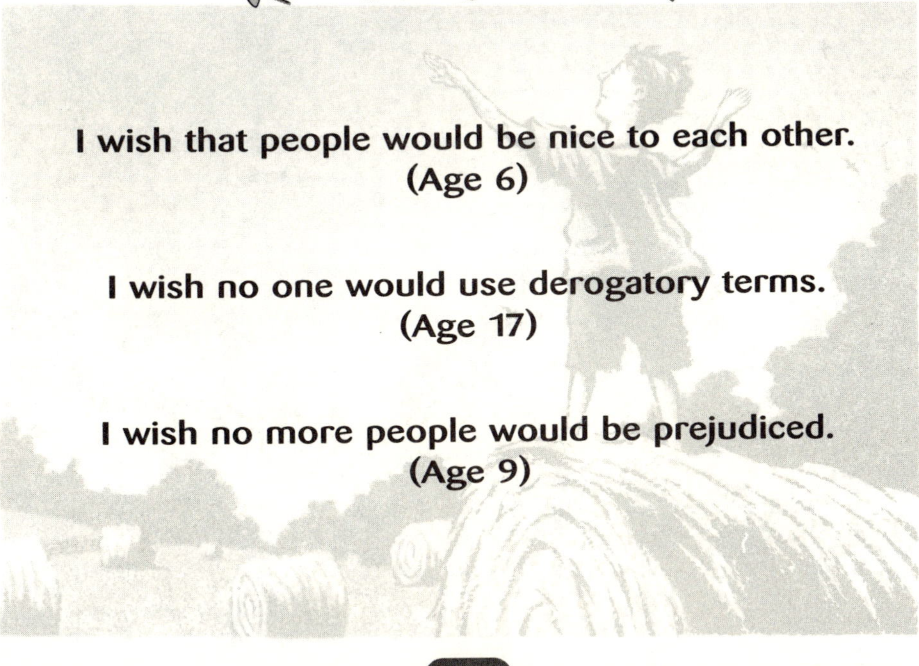

I wish that people would be nice to each other.
(Age 6)

I wish no one would use derogatory terms.
(Age 17)

I wish no more people would be prejudiced.
(Age 9)

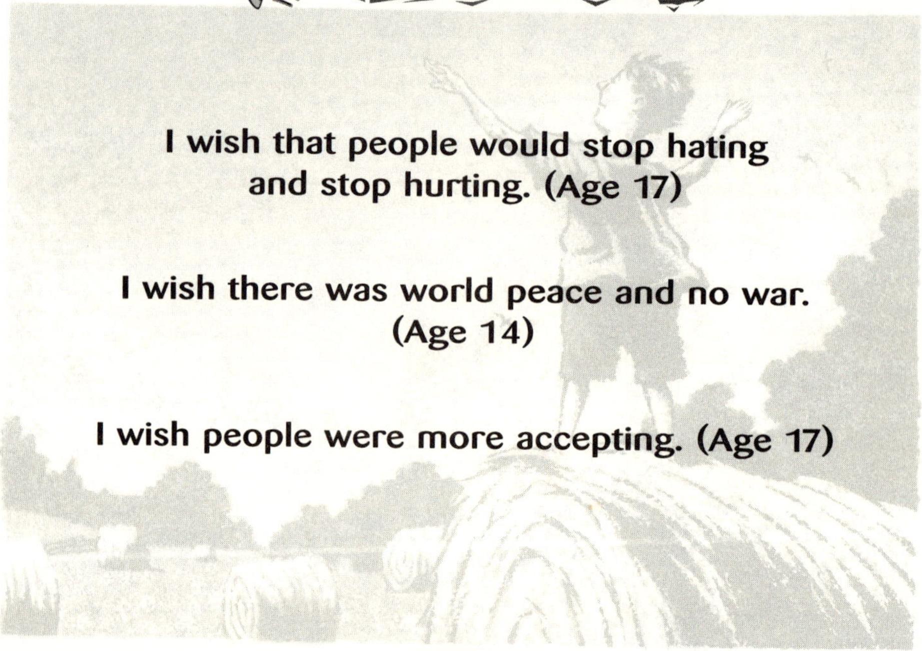

I wish that people would stop hating and stop hurting. (Age 17)

I wish there was world peace and no war. (Age 14)

I wish people were more accepting. (Age 17)

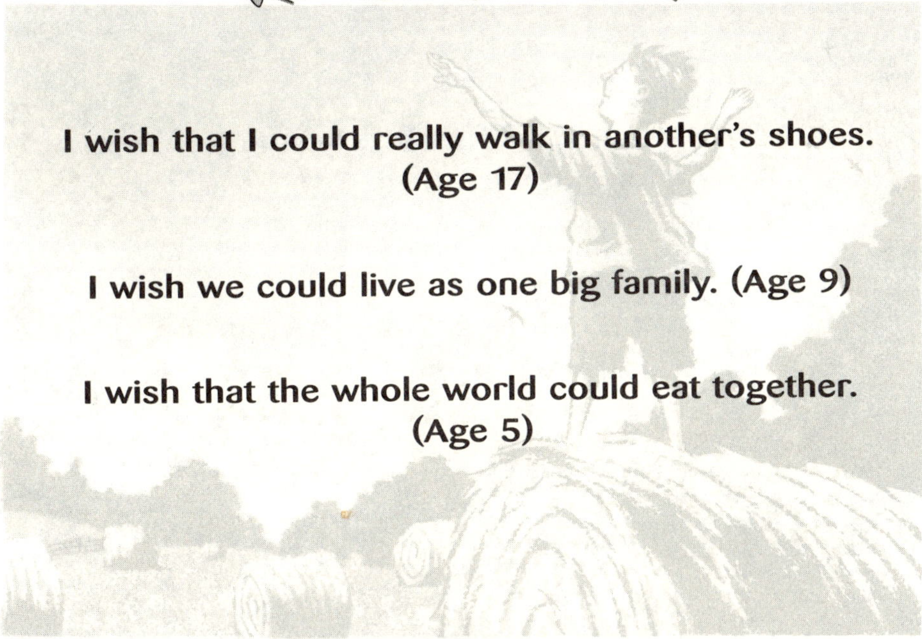

I wish that I could really walk in another's shoes. (Age 17)

I wish we could live as one big family. (Age 9)

I wish that the whole world could eat together. (Age 5)

I wish I did not spend so much time thinking about why. (Age 18)

I wish not that I could change the past, but that I could be content with it and live with fewer regrets. (Age 17)

I wish I was at a birthday party. (Age 5)

I wish my birthday was today. (Age 5)

I wish that every day was my birthday. (Age 5)

I wish there were more holidays. (Age 9)

I wish I had a year's supply of my grandma's delicious chocolate sheet cake. (Age 12)

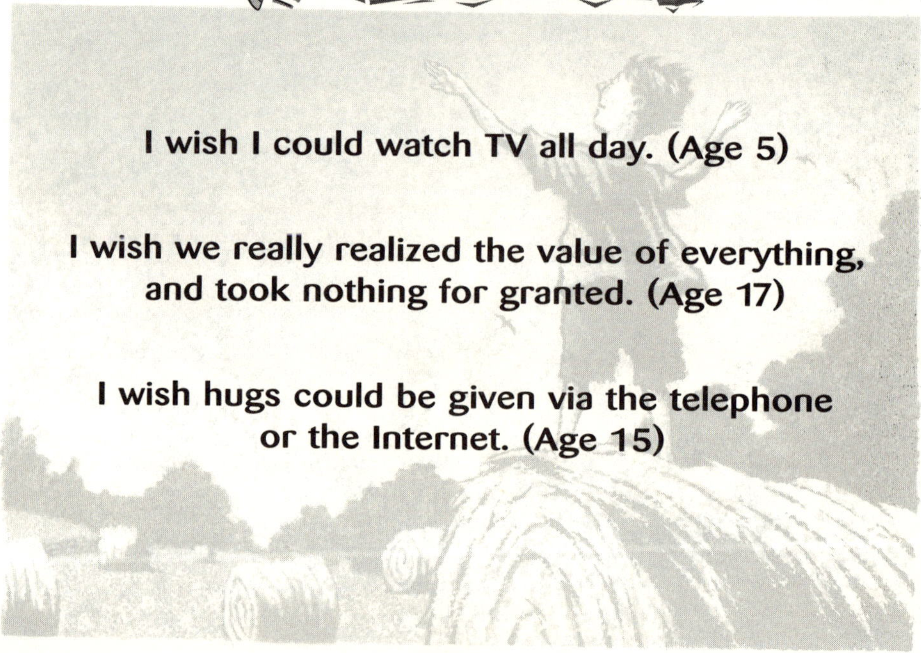

I wish I could watch TV all day. (Age 5)

I wish we really realized the value of everything, and took nothing for granted. (Age 17)

I wish hugs could be given via the telephone or the Internet. (Age 15)

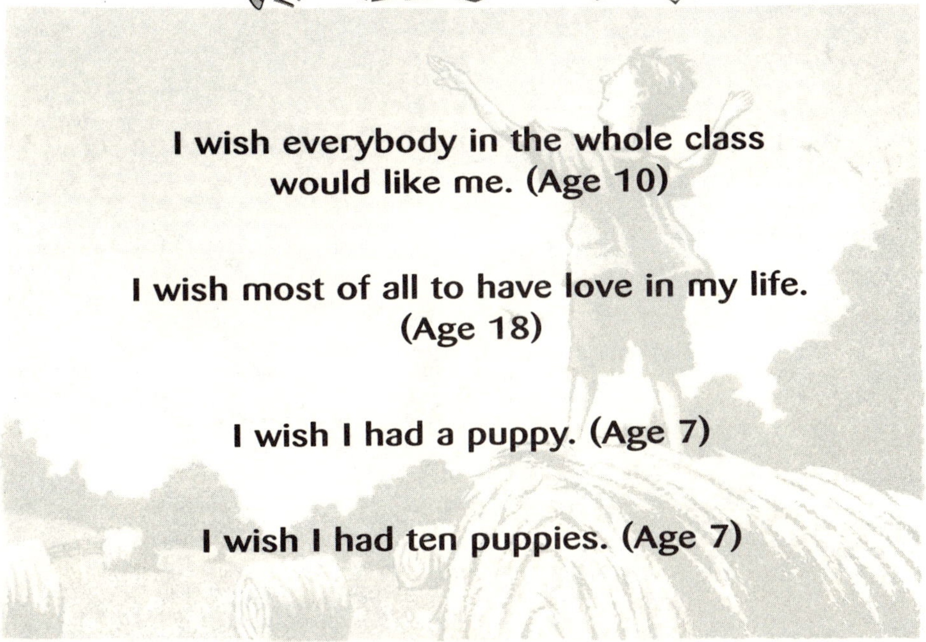

I wish everybody in the whole class would like me. (Age 10)

I wish most of all to have love in my life. (Age 18)

I wish I had a puppy. (Age 7)

I wish I had ten puppies. (Age 7)

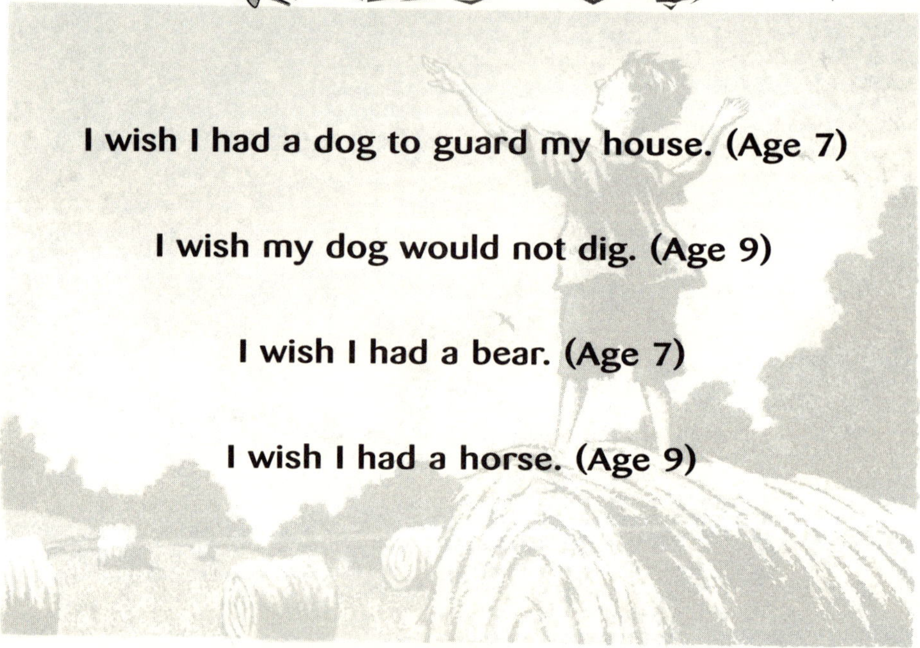

I wish I had a dog to guard my house. (Age 7)

I wish my dog would not dig. (Age 9)

I wish I had a bear. (Age 7)

I wish I had a horse. (Age 9)

I wish I could have a rat and a rabbit. (Age 10)

I wish that birdies weren't afraid of me so I could hold them. (Age 5)

I wish I could buy a BB gun. (Age 8)

I wish that the bad people wouldn't take our house away. (Age 5)

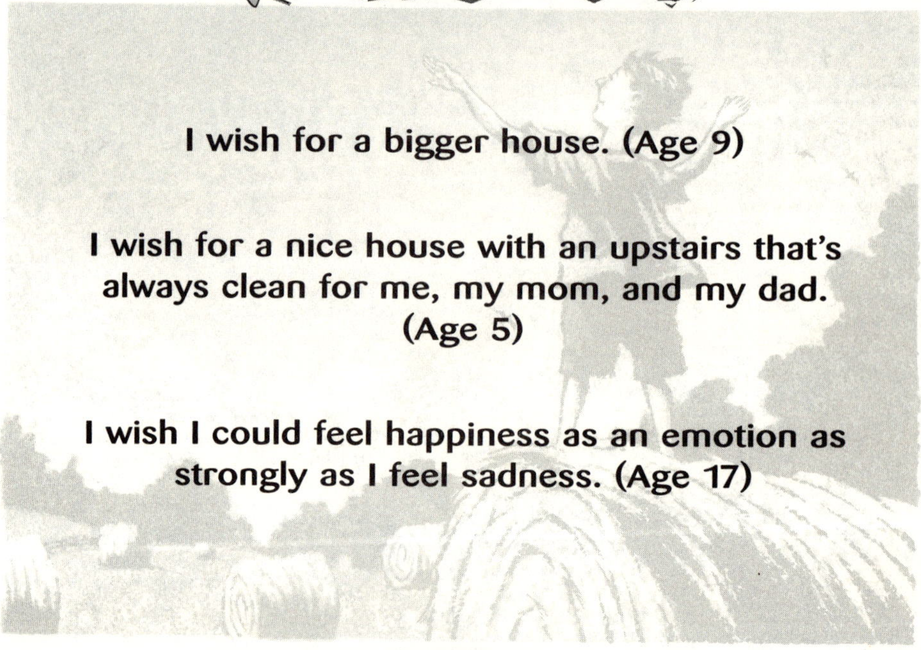

I wish for a bigger house. (Age 9)

I wish for a nice house with an upstairs that's always clean for me, my mom, and my dad. (Age 5)

I wish I could feel happiness as an emotion as strongly as I feel sadness. (Age 17)

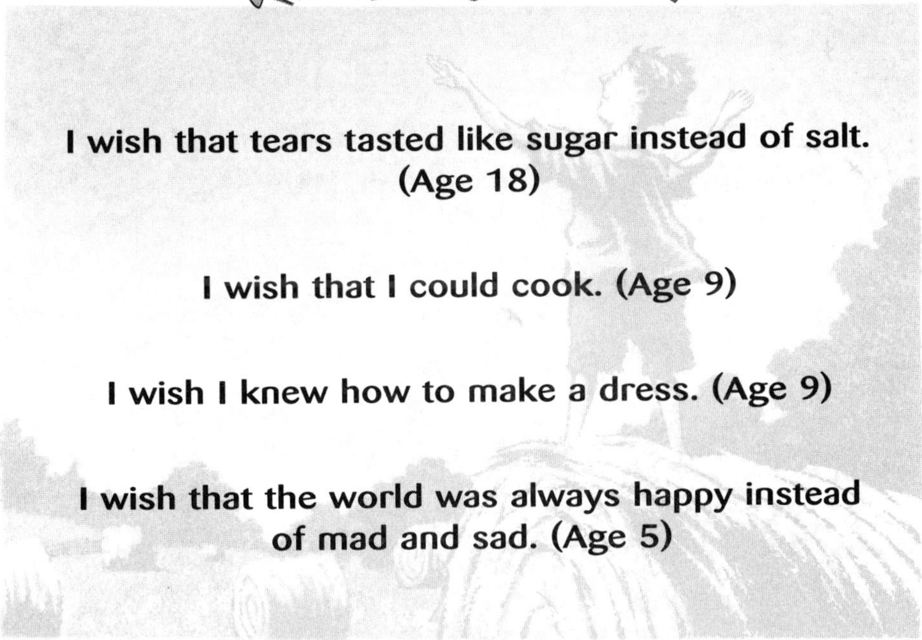

I wish that tears tasted like sugar instead of salt. (Age 18)

I wish that I could cook. (Age 9)

I wish I knew how to make a dress. (Age 9)

I wish that the world was always happy instead of mad and sad. (Age 5)

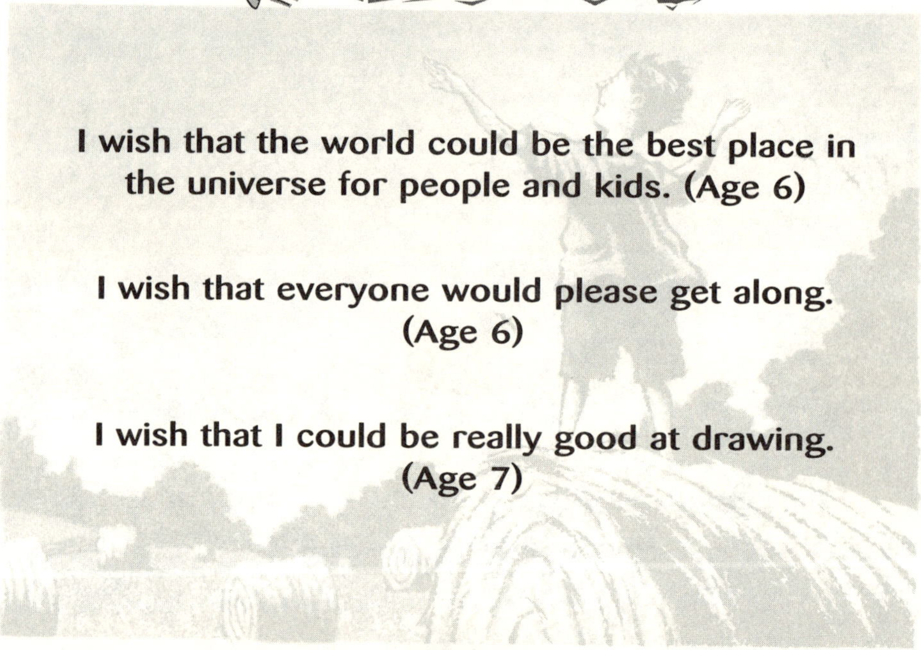

I wish that the world could be the best place in the universe for people and kids. (Age 6)

I wish that everyone would please get along. (Age 6)

I wish that I could be really good at drawing. (Age 7)

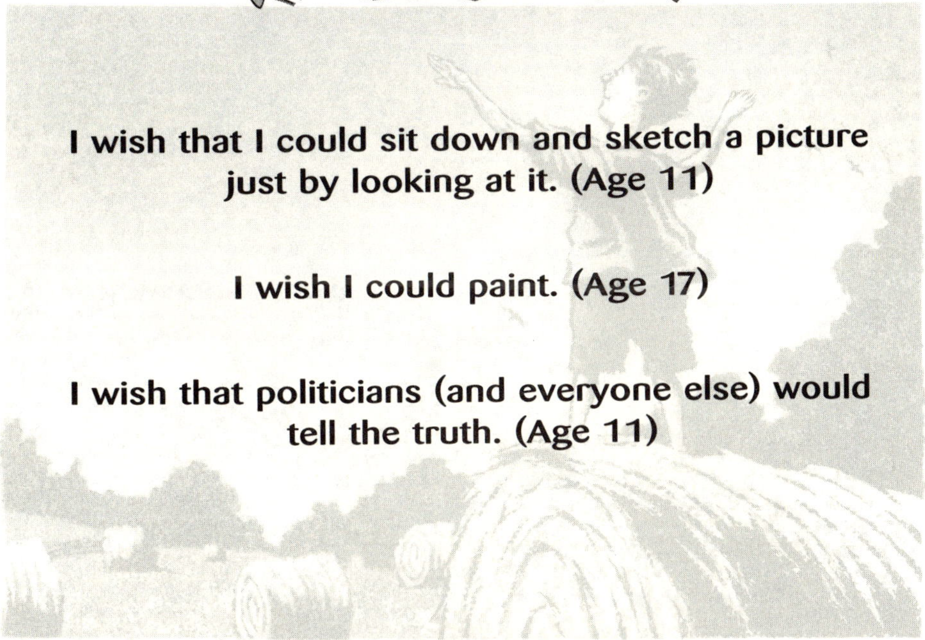

I wish that I could sit down and sketch a picture just by looking at it. (Age 11)

I wish I could paint. (Age 17)

I wish that politicians (and everyone else) would tell the truth. (Age 11)

I wish that everyone would follow the rules. (Age 6)

I wish there were no more bad guys because they steal stuff. (Age 6)

I wish that late to bed, late to rise makes a man healthy, wealthy, and wise. (Age 16)

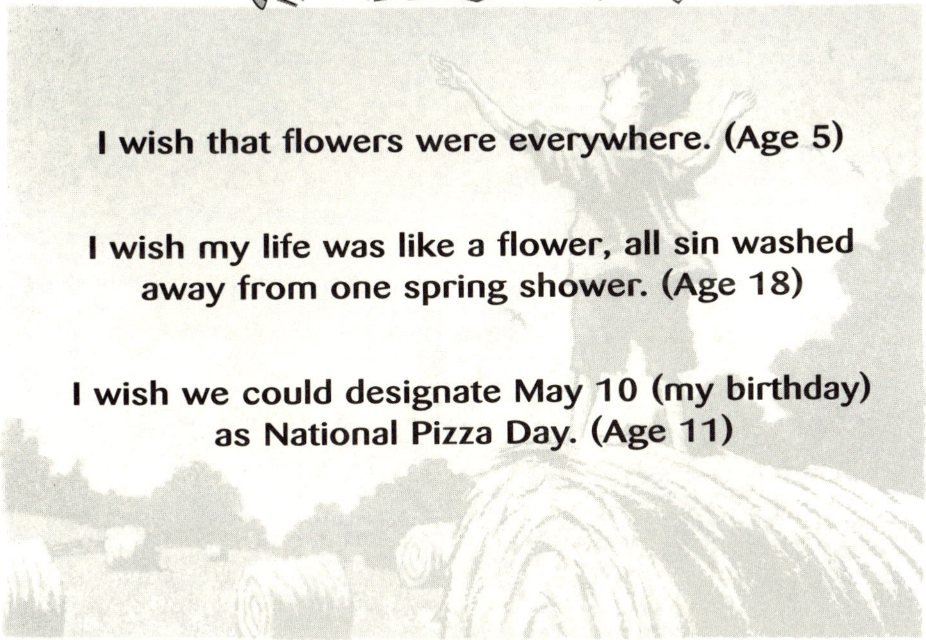

I wish that flowers were everywhere. (Age 5)

I wish my life was like a flower, all sin washed away from one spring shower. (Age 18)

I wish we could designate May 10 (my birthday) as National Pizza Day. (Age 11)

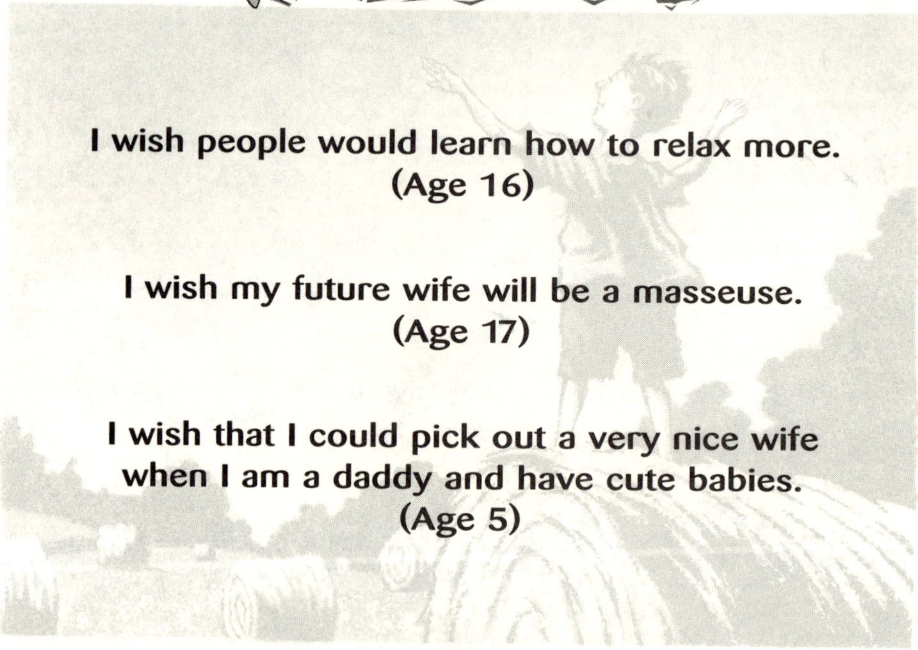

I wish people would learn how to relax more.
(Age 16)

I wish my future wife will be a masseuse.
(Age 17)

I wish that I could pick out a very nice wife
when I am a daddy and have cute babies.
(Age 5)

I wish I wouldn't have to be worried before a test or on Report Card Day. (Age 11)

I wish I wouldn't worry before a recital or performance. (Age 11)

I wish I could run faster so I could keep up with life. (Age 12)

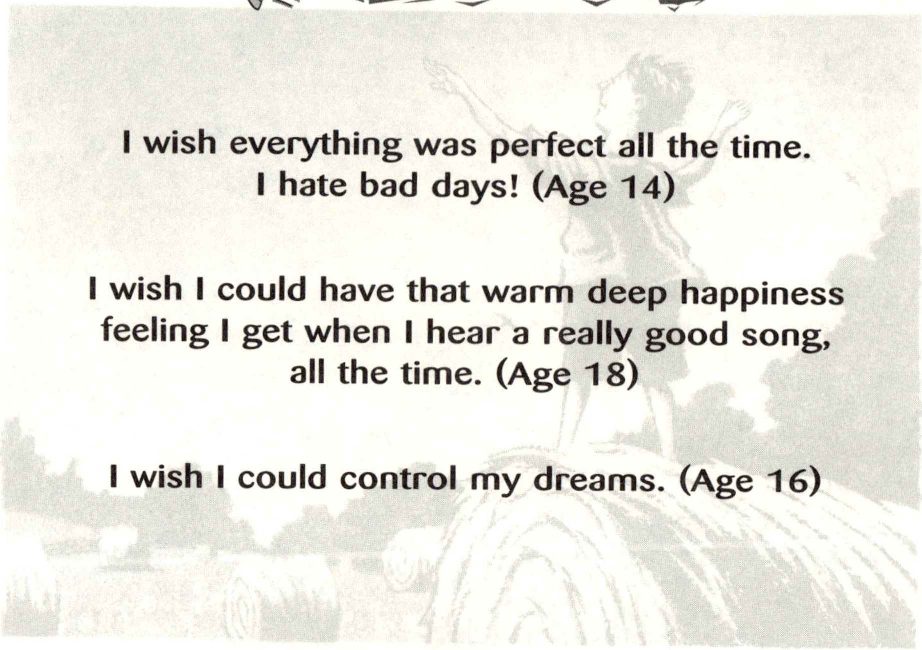

I wish everything was perfect all the time.
I hate bad days! (Age 14)

I wish I could have that warm deep happiness feeling I get when I hear a really good song, all the time. (Age 18)

I wish I could control my dreams. (Age 16)

I wish my dream would come true. (Age 5)

I wish that I will be a happy adult. (Age 11)

I wish that there would be less suffering in the world, not just physically, but emotionally. (Age 12)

I wish the world was made of food, then no one would be hungry. (Age 7)

I wish that everyone would share, and that we could all play together. (Age 5)

I wish that the whole world could be friends. (Age 5)

I wish for a life full of good times. (Age 18)

I wish that wishes did come true. (Age 16)